TAKE-HOME BOOKS

HARCOURT SCIENCE

BOOKS

Harcourt School Publishers

Orlando • Boston • Dallas • Chicago • San Diego

www.harcourtschool.com

HARCOURT SCIENCE
Contents

UNIT A   **TH1–16**

Chapter 1	Classifying Animals	TH1
Chapter 2	Animal Adaptations	TH5
Chapter 3	Plant Adaptations	TH9
Chapter 4	Human Body Systems	TH13

UNIT B   **TH17–28**

Chapter 1	Looking at Ecosystems	TH17
Chapter 2	Soil Conservation	TH21
Chapter 3	Protecting Ecosystems	TH25

UNIT C   **TH29–40**

Chapter 1	Volcanoes	TH29
Chapter 2	Minerals and Rocks	TH33
Chapter 3	Fossils—The Petrified Forest	TH37

UNIT D   **TH41–52**

Chapter 1	Wind	TH41
Chapter 2	Mapping the Ocean Floor	TH45
Chapter 3	Life Cycle of a Star	TH49

UNIT E   **TH53–68**

Chapter 1	Sink or Swim—Life Jackets and How They Work	TH53
Chapter 2	Insulation	TH57
Chapter 3	How Animals Use Sound	TH61
Chapter 4	Electricity and Magnetism in Transportation	TH65

UNIT F   **TH69–76**

Chapter 1	How Rockets Work	TH69
Chapter 2	How Gears Work	TH73

About the Take-Home Books

These delightful books are designed to extend the content in the *Harcourt Science* Pupil Edition. There is one Take-Home Book for every chapter in the Pupil Edition. Although the Take-Home Books are intended to supplement *Harcourt Science,* they can also be used independently of the program.

Each Take-Home Book contains

▶ Fast Facts—high-interest facts to engage students in the topic.

▶ Feature Story—content to extend and enrich the content in the Pupil Edition chapter. This section of the book can be used to reinforce grade-level reading skills.

▶ Hands-On Activity—a science investigation students can do at home or school. Materials required for the activity are usually household items.

▶ Vocabulary Fun—puzzles and activities that provide reinforcement of the vocabulary introduced in the feature story.

▶ Science Fun—new information, puzzles, riddles, and cartoons to bring closure to each topic.

Take-Home Books are intended to be copied and sent home with students at the end of each chapter. However, you may wish to distribute the books in class and have students work on them in small groups. Some of the topics in the Take-Home Books lend themselves to further study as part of a class or individual science fair project.

The Take-Home Books provide family support. Students can take them home to read with family members. They can also involve family members in hands-on activities, vocabulary reinforcement, and science fun!

To assemble a Take-Home Book, first photocopy the master pages so that they contain the front and back side of the page, just as it appears in this book. Then, fold the pages and assemble them so the eight pages of the Take-Home Book are in order.

Science Fun

Interesting Insects

Insects are among the most fascinating species on Earth. They smell mostly with their antennae, and some even taste with their feet. Many insects sense vibrations through the hair on their bodies. Insects have no voices, and yet some can be heard about 1.6 kilometers (1 mi) away. Many insects have enormous strength. An ant can lift something that is 50 times its own weight. If a 36-kilogram (about 80-lb) girl could do the same, she would be able to lift something that weighed 1800 kilograms (about 4000 lb)!

JOKE TIME

▶ **Q:** What took Cinderella Insect to the Prince's Ball?

A: *a golden roach*

▶ **Q:** What do the insects use to mend their clothes?

A: *beetle and thread*

▶ **Q:** Why wasn't the spider invited to run in the insect marathon?

A: *because he'd always be a leg or two ahead*

Answers to Ant Life Cycle: A. larva, B. pupa, C. adult

Answers to Vocabulary Fun: 1. Classification, 2. kingdom, 3. species, 4. arthropods

CLASSIFYING ANIMALS

Insects

Fold

FAST FACT
About 1 million insect species have been discovered so far. About 7000 to 10,000 new insect species are discovered each year.

FAST FACT
The smallest insects are less than 0.025 cm (0.01 in.) long. The largest ones are almost 30 cm (1 ft) long.

FAST FACT
It takes some insects 13 to 17 years to reach adulthood. The common housefly reaches adulthood in about ten days.

INSECTS

Have you ever swatted a fly? Most people try to get rid of insects. Some insects bite us. Some land on our food. Some gnaw on flowers and vegetables in our gardens. But without insects, people could not survive. Plants need insects, and people need plants (or animals that eat plants) for food.

Insects spread pollen from flower to flower, which helps plants reproduce. Insects also help turn the soil near plant roots, which helps plants take in oxygen and water.

Classifying Insects

The table below shows how scientists classify insects. Look at the table. What characteristic is the basis for the classification?

INSECTS

Winged Insects	Wingless Insects
bee	weevil
dragonfly	beetle
wasp	flea

VocabularyFun

Fill in the blanks with the words below to complete the rhymes.

classification   arthropods   kingdom   species

1. Grouping living things is my game.
   _____ is my name.

2. The largest group of living things
   Is a _____ with neither land nor kings.

3. Divide a kingdom in parts we call
   _____, the smallest groups of all.

4. The _____' legs have several joints.
   Their bodies have segments at different points.

Life Cycle of an Ant

Label the stages of life for the ant. Use the words in the box.

adult	pupa	larva

Answers on page 8

Harcourt

BE AN INSECT DETECTIVE

Do this activity to locate and observe some insects that live near you.

MATERIALS

▶ hand lens (optional)
▶ pencil   ▶ notebook
▶ crayons or colored pencils

PROCEDURE

CAUTION: Be careful not to investigate fire ants or any stinging insects.

1. Decide the best place to find insects. Go outside and observe them. Use a hand lens if you have one.
2. Make a rough sketch of the insects and the place where you found them. Then go inside and make your final drawing.
3. If it's too cold to observe insects outside, you can draw insects that you have seen in warmer weather.

CONCLUSIONS

What types of insects live near you? If you don't know, ask an adult or look in a book to find out.

Unit A • Chapter 1   TH3

AN INSECT'S LIFE CYCLE

Like all animals, insects move through stages, called a life cycle, as they grow and change. The drawing shows the life cycle of an ant.

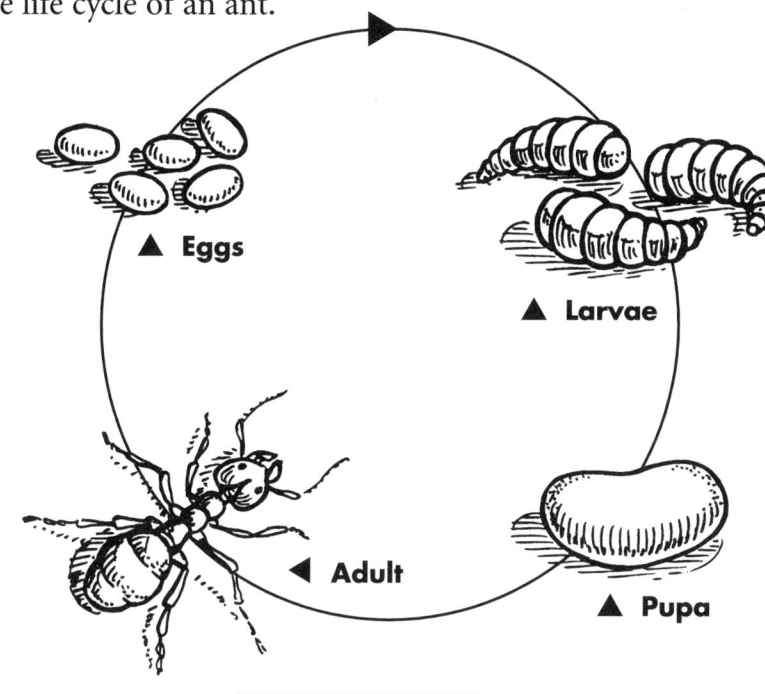

▲ Eggs   ▲ Larvae   ◀ Adult   ▲ Pupa

Find Out

What is the life cycle of a grasshopper? Use reference books, computers, or encyclopedias to find the answer. Then make a drawing of a grasshopper's life cycle.

THE INSECT BODY PLAN

All adult insects have bodies made up of three parts: the head, thorax, and abdomen. Find these three body parts of a grasshopper in the drawing below.

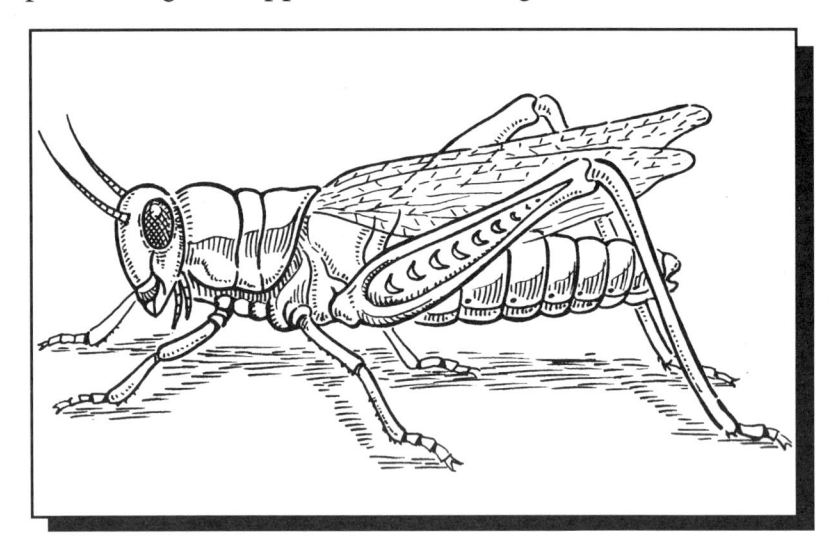

Classify the grasshopper. In which group of insects, wingless or winged, does it belong?

Make a model of a grasshopper or other insect. You can use materials such as chenille stems, clay, wax paper, buttons or sequins, toothpicks, and construction paper.

SOCIAL INSECTS

Some insect species are called social insects because they live in organized groups. The honeybee is a social insect. It lives in a community called a hive, made up of one queen, drones, and thousands of worker bees. The queen and her workers act as a team to raise new honeybees and care for the community.

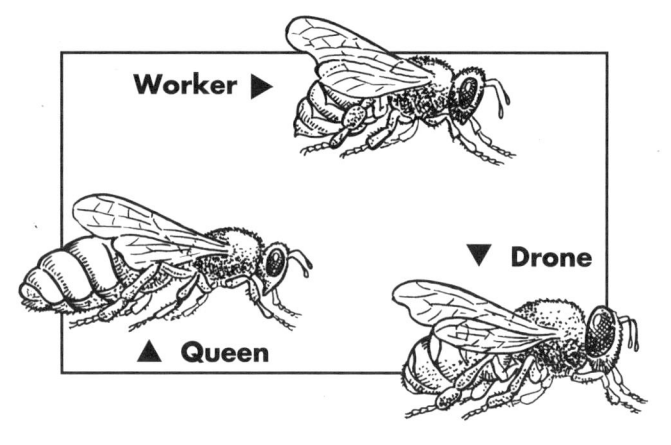

Worker ▶

▲ Queen

▼ Drone

The queen is the mother of all the bees. Her job is laying eggs—often more than 1500 per day.

As their name tells you, the worker bees do the work. They gather and store food. They build the honeycomb. They make the honey. They clean and defend the hive.

The drone honeybees help in reproduction. After mating with the queen, a drone immediately dies.

Science Fun

The Atlantic puffin is brightly colored in the summer breeding season and duller in winter. The drawings below show an Atlantic puffin in summer and in winter. Color the puffins to show how they look in each season. Use the tips below to help you, or find photographs in a book or encyclopedia.

▶ In breeding season the tip of the bill is red and the base is blue-gray outlined in yellow. There is a red ring around the eye. The legs and webbed feet are orange. The face and front of the puffin are white. The back of the puffin is black.

▶ In winter the tip of the bill is a dull yellow. The eye has no red ring around it. The face of the puffin is gray. Its front and back, while still black and white, are duller and grayer than in breeding season.

Answers to Vocabulary Fun: A. ocean, B. fish, C. salt gland, D. land, E. North Atlantic

Fold

ANIMAL ADAPTATIONS

Puffins

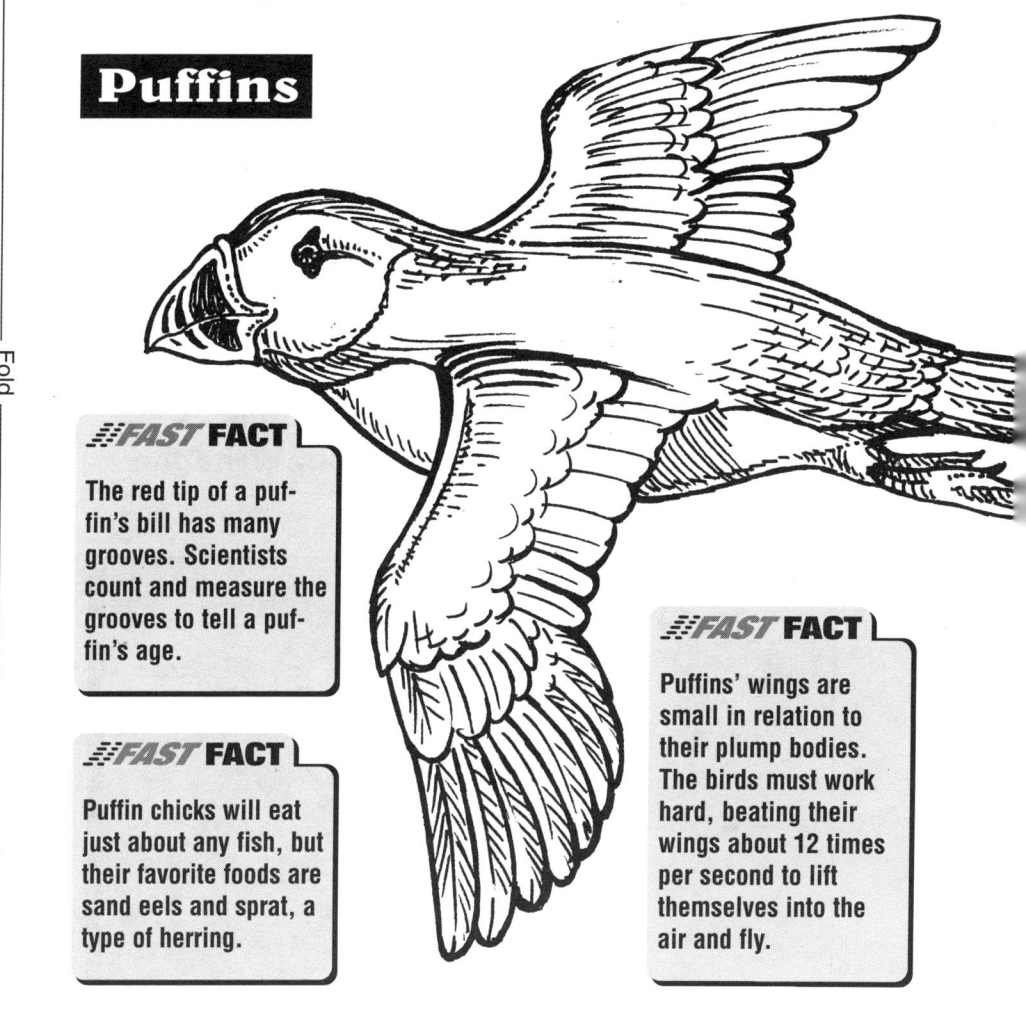

FAST FACT

The red tip of a puffin's bill has many grooves. Scientists count and measure the grooves to tell a puffin's age.

FAST FACT

Puffin chicks will eat just about any fish, but their favorite foods are sand eels and sprat, a type of herring.

FAST FACT

Puffins' wings are small in relation to their plump bodies. The birds must work hard, beating their wings about 12 times per second to lift themselves into the air and fly.

PUFFINS

Puffins, like all animals, live in an environment where they can meet their needs for oxygen, food, water, and shelter. Puffins are sea birds. A key part of their environment is the ocean. Puffins gather in ocean areas where fish feed because fish are, by far, the greatest part of the puffin diet.

Think & Do

The map below shows where Atlantic puffins are found. How would you describe these places—inland, along the coast, or in the sea? Use an atlas to find the names of places where Atlantic puffins are found. Write the place names on the map.

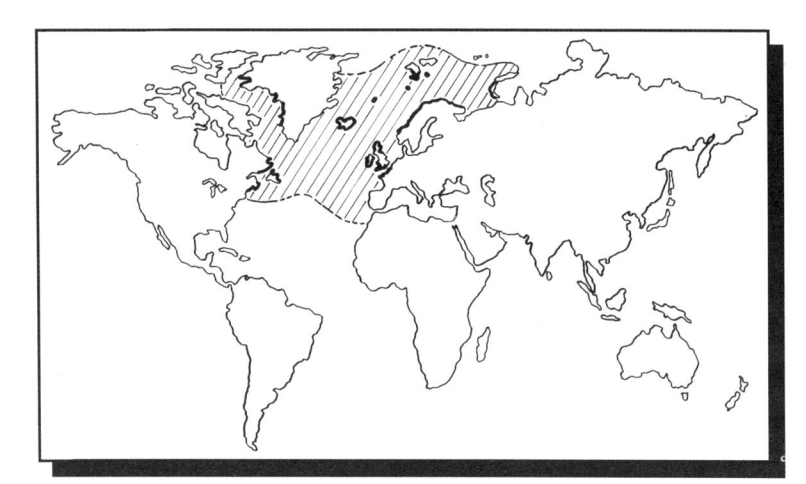

2 • Take-Home Book

VocabularyFun

Use the words in the Word Bank to fill in the circles around the puffin. Choose a term that best matches the label in the circle.

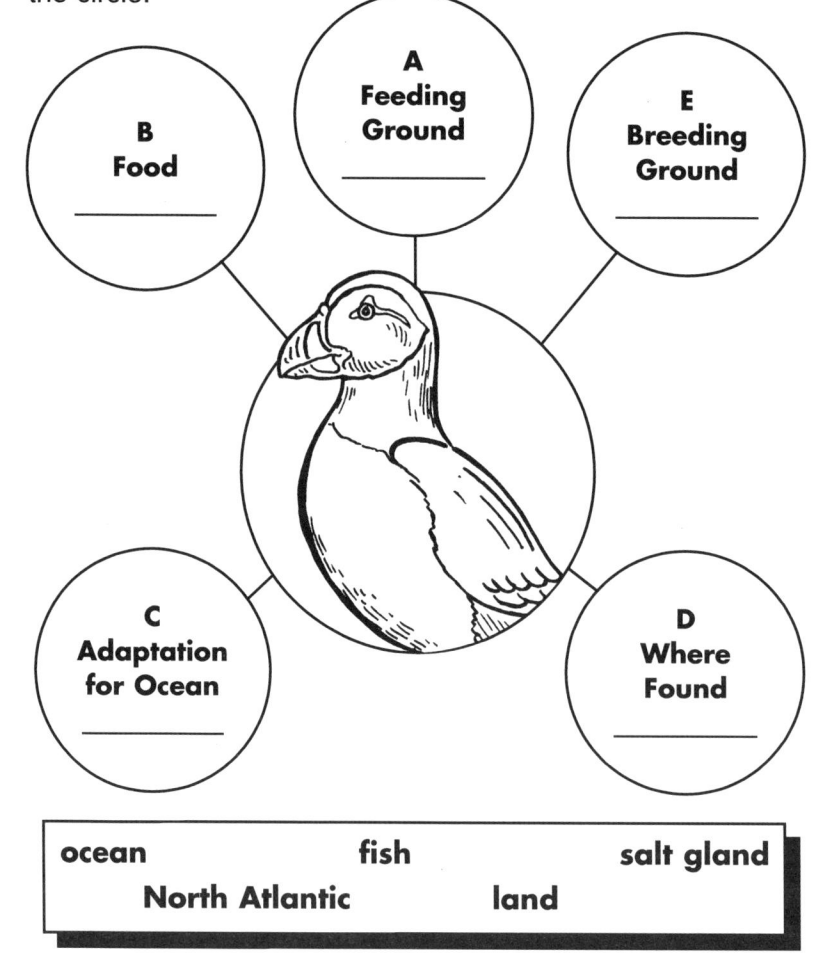

A
Feeding
Ground
_____

B
Food
_____

E
Breeding
Ground
_____

C
Adaptation
for Ocean
_____

D
Where
Found
_____

ocean	fish	salt gland
North Atlantic	land	

Answers on page 8

WATERPROOF FEATHERS

How does the oil released by a puffin's glands help it stay dry?

MATERIALS

▶ **2 cotton rags**

▶ **cooking oil**

▶ **water**

▶ **dropper**

PROCEDURE

1. Lay both rags on a kitchen counter or table. With your fingers, coat the top side of one rag with oil.
2. Gently place one drop of water on the unoiled rag. Observe what happens.
3. Place one drop of water on the oiled rag, and observe. What happens?
4. Repeat two times on each rag. Are your results the same each time?

CONCLUSIONS

Which rag, oiled or unoiled, did the drop of water soak through more slowly? Why? Think about the oil released by a puffin's glands onto its feathers. How does the oil help the puffin stay dry?

PUFFIN ADAPTATIONS

Puffins have adaptations that allow them to meet their needs in the ocean, where they spend most of each year, and on land, where they hatch and raise their young.

How does a puffin keep from getting so wet that it sinks? One sea bird adaptation is large oil glands. These glands release oil that waterproofs the puffins' feathers.

Have you ever gotten ocean water in your mouth or nose? If so, you probably spit it out because it was salty. Puffins can drink ocean water because of an adaptation called a salt

gland. This gland allows the puffin to comfortably release through its nose the salt that it swallows in ocean water.

Where do most birds build nests? In trees. The puffin does not. It makes burrows in the ground. Two adaptations, sharp beaks and broad webbed feet, allow the puffin to dig into the ground and push the loosened earth aside.

BREEDING SEASON

Each year, in the late winter or spring, puffins return from the open sea to the waters around their burrows. It is breeding season.

Male and female puffins choose mates. They nibble on each other's brightly colored bills, stretching up and down in a kind of dance.

The female puffin lays one large egg at the end of a burrow. She and her mate take turns keeping the egg warm. After the egg hatches, the parents work hard to feed their chick, making four or five trips to bring food from the sea to the burrow each day.

Find Out

Puffins can carry in their mouths up to 28 fish or up to 50 sand eels at one time. How can they carry such a load? Use reference books, computers, or encyclopedias to find out. Compare your findings with those of a classmate.

IN THE AIR OR UNDER THE WATER

Puffins' wings have adaptations for moving in water and air. The birds dive and swim underwater to find food. The small size of their wings is good for swimming.

This puffin is returning from a successful hunt to its burrow. Notice how the puffin has spread its tail feathers, for help in braking as it lands.

A chick is a downy soft gray. It isn't long until the young puffin struggles down to the water and swims away. But it must avoid sea gulls, which eat puffins.

The chicks prepare to leave the burrows by practicing at night when sea gulls are asleep. Then, when the moon is new and the night is at its darkest, the chicks half fly and half tumble down into the water. They swim as far from land as they can before dawn.

Science Fun

An Orchid Myth

Most people think of orchids as flowers that grow in the jungle. This is not true. Orchids can be found all over the world. Some orchids grow in hot, low coastal regions of the tropics, while others grow in the highest mountains of the Himalayas. Orchids are found in bogs, swamps, treetops, rocks, and sand dunes. There are even three Australian species that grow underground!

WHERE DO ORCHIDS GET THEIR NAME?

Sometimes a plant gets its name because of the shape of its flowers. See if you can guess the names of these three orchids.

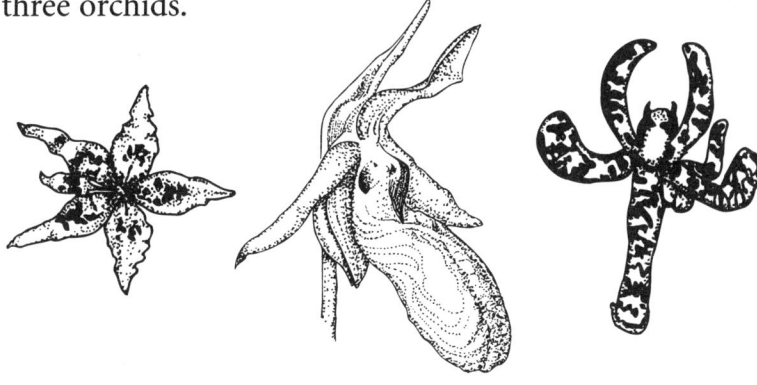

a. _____ b. _____ c. _____

Answers to Science Fun: a. star orchid, b. lady slipper orchid, c. scorpion orchid

Answers to Vocabulary Fun: 1. pseudobulb, 2. pedicel, 3. pollinate, 4. reproduce, 5. orchid, 6. mimicry, 7. root, 8. pollen, 9. sepal

PLANT ADAPTATIONS

Tree-Growing Orchids

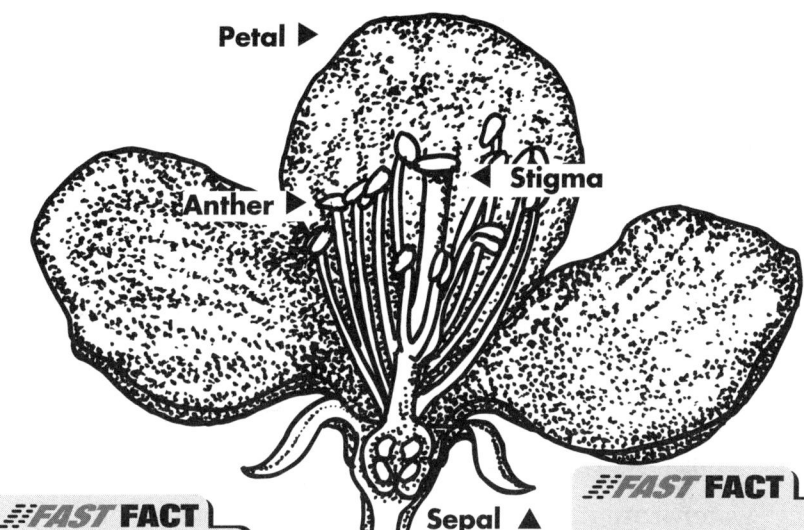

Petal ▶

Anther ▶   ◀ Stigma

Sepal ▲

FAST FACT

In the 1600s, explorers and traders from Europe discovered tree-growing orchids in Jamaica, the Spice Islands, New Guinea, and the Philippines.

FAST FACT

A single orchid seed-pod may produce as many as two million seeds.

FAST FACT

Many orchid species "trick" insects into helping them reproduce. On some orchids, flies go through a tunnel where they get covered with pollen.

ORCHID
ADAPTATIONS

About half of Earth's 15,000 to 25,000 orchid species grow on the ground. The other half are *epiphytes* (EP•uh•fyts), or air plants. They grow on tall trees in regions where it rains nearly every day.

You must look up high to see epiphytes like these blooming in the wild. These orchids grow at the tops of trees, where they can get the sunlight and air they need to live.

Orchids also need water. Tree-growing orchids get water from dew, rain, and moisture on the surface of the tree. Two adaptations, thick leaves and pseudobulbs (SOO•doh•buhlbz), or false bulbs, enable orchids to store moisture when the weather is dry.

Fold

Vocabulary Fun

Unscramble these words to fit the blanks. The boxed letters make the word that tells the theme of this booklet.

sepal	pedicel	mimicry
pseudobulb	reproduce	pollen
pollinate	orchid	root

1. lbdoubpseu __ __ e __ __ __ __ __ __ __
2. cdlpeei p __ __ __ __ __ __
3. illonpate __ __ __ __ i __ __ __
4. dropreuec __ __ p __ __ __ __ __
5. dochri __ __ __ h __ __
6. cyrimim __ __ __ __ __ __ y
7. otor __ __ __ t
8. lonpel __ __ __ __ e __
9. splae s __ __ __ __

Answers on page 8

AIR AND EARTH PLANTS

How is an epiphyte similar to and different from plants in your home or neighborhood? Do this activity to find out.

MATERIALS

▶ **notebook**

▶ **pencil with eraser**

PROCEDURE

1. Review the drawings of orchids in this booklet. Then examine flowers that grow outdoors and inside your home to see how they are the same as and different from orchids. Notice how your flowers get air, nutrients, light, and water. Draw or write your observations.

2. Think about what the outdoor flowers look like when they are blooming. Have you noticed insects, birds, or other small animals brushing against the flowers? What does that suggest?

CONCLUSIONS

In what ways are flowers where you live like an orchid? In what ways are they different? Draw or write your response.

NUTRIENTS

Tree-growing orchids get nutrients from bits of dust that settle on them and from decaying leaves in the tree branches. Remember that plants take in nutrients (and water) mainly through their roots. Most plant roots are protected by soil. The roots of tree-growing orchids are not protected. They are always exposed to air. Tree-growing orchids have fleshy roots with a white coating called *velamen*, which enables them to withstand constant exposure.

Think & Do

Find the pedicel (PED•ih•suhl) of the orchid shown on page 1. A flower starts growing upright on the pedicel. As it grows, the pedicel rotates 180 degrees. Which way does the flower face when it blossoms? To find out, use your palm as the pedicel and measure a turn of 180 degrees with a protractor.

POLLEN MOVERS

Orchids reproduce from seeds. For seeds to form, grains of pollen must move from the male to the female parts of an orchid. Tree-growing orchids have amazing adaptations that get insects and birds to move the pollen.

This orchid smells good to bees. A bee moves toward the good smell. It lands on the flower and scratches the surface. The scratching releases a chemical that the bee absorbs. The chemical makes the bee drunk!

The drunken bee falls down a slide where it picks up pollen. That way the pollen moves—on the bee—to the next orchid.

MIMICRY

Orchids like this are known as yellow bee orchids because their yellow and brown colors make them look like bees. This is an example of mimicry. A light breeze makes the orchids move like an angry swarm. Real bees attack the orchids to protect their territory. They pollinate the flowers as they strike them.

This orchid is the fastest gun in the West—or at least in the world of orchids. The male flower gives off a 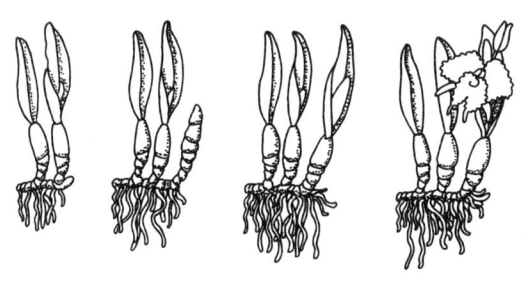 musky smell that attracts bees. When a bee touches the flower's hair-trigger, the flower shoots the bee with sticky grains of pollen.

Find Out

How do other tree-growing orchids get insects to move pollen? Use reference books or encyclopedias to find the answer. Draw a picture with labels that shows how an orchid not in this booklet gets insects to move pollen.

Science Fun

Excercise Helps

Exercise and activities can help the body to be fit and healthy. They can build strength, flexibility, and a stronger heart. Below is a chart with a list of activities under each heading. In each column, color the box that names your favorite activity. Add activities you like that are not listed.

STRENGTH	FLEXIBILITY	STRONGER HEART
climbing	gymnastics	running
monkey bars	tumbling	swimming
tug-of-war	ballet	walking
chin-ups	yoga	riding a bicycle
tennis		soccer
throwing balls		jumping rope

Answers to Vocabulary Fun: 1. nicotine, 2. nutrients, 3. alcohol, 4. tobacco, 5. Food Guide Pyramid, 6. carbohydrates

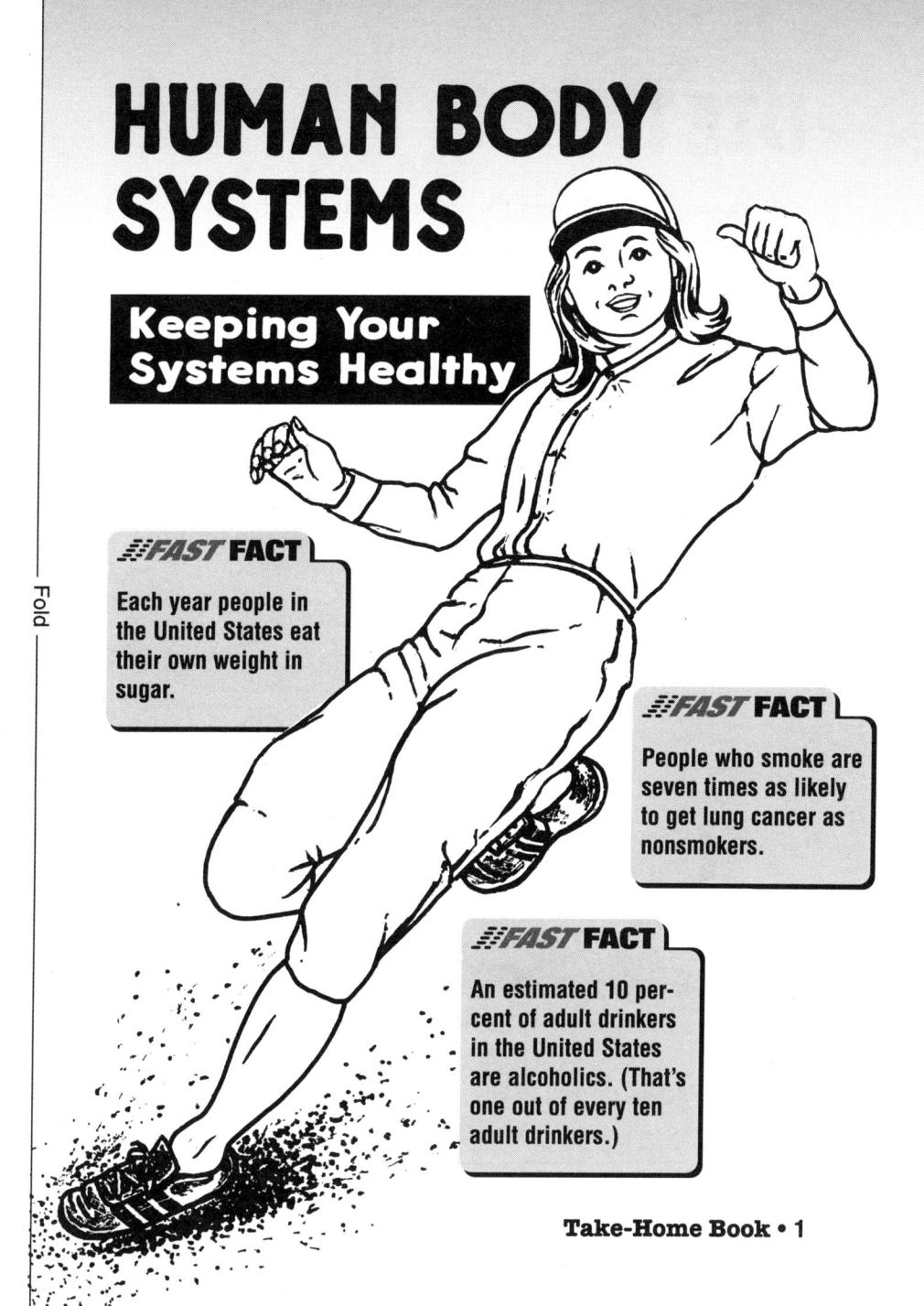

HUMAN BODY SYSTEMS

Keeping Your Systems Healthy

FAST FACT
Each year people in the United States eat their own weight in sugar.

FAST FACT
People who smoke are seven times as likely to get lung cancer as nonsmokers.

FAST FACT
An estimated 10 percent of adult drinkers in the United States are alcoholics. (That's one out of every ten adult drinkers.)

DIET

Perhaps you've heard the expression "Garbage in, garbage out." The expression started with computers, but it can also be applied to your body. A healthful diet is important for a healthy body. If you eat "garbage," your systems will produce "garbage" when you need to think hard about a problem or run fast to catch a bus. If you eat healthful foods, your systems will work for you to build and maintain a sharp mind and strong body. The Food Guide Pyramid, shown below, shows the building blocks of a healthful diet.

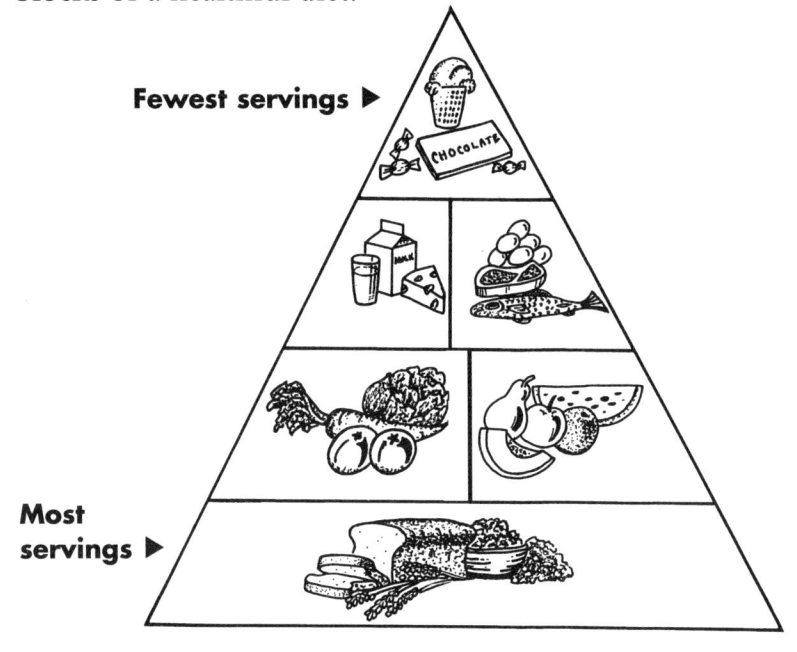

Fewest servings ▶

Most servings ▶

VocabularyFun

| tobacco | nicotine | alcohol | nutrients |
| carbohydrates | | Food Guide Pyramid | |

RIDDLES

Use the words from the vocabulary list to answer the riddles. Write each answer on the line.

1. I am a poisonous chemical obtained by smoking. What am I? _____

2. I am the substances found in food that are good for you. What am I? _____

3. I am sometimes called booze. What am I? _____

4. I am sometimes smoked by students to make them feel grown up. What am I? _____

5. People use me to help them choose a healthful eating plan. What am I? _____

6. I am a terrific source of energy. What am I? _____

Answers on page 8

PREPARE A HEALTHFUL SNACK

Do this activity to make a healthful and tasty snack for you and your family.

MATERIALS

▶ **foods and drinks from your pantry and refrigerator**

▶ **serving utensils**

PROCEDURE

1. Ask an adult for permission to use the kitchen and prepare a snack. **CAUTION: Do not use foods that must be heated. Ask an adult for help if you need to cut or slice anything.**

2. Look in your kitchen for ingredients that could be used to make a healthful and tasty snack. Be creative. You could use lowfat flavored yogurt as a dip for fresh fruit. You could make a healthful soft drink by mixing apple or grape juice and club soda.

3. Prepare the snack and enjoy it.

CONCLUSIONS

What foods and drinks did you choose to make a healthful snack? What foods or drinks did you rule out because they were less healthful?

Fold

SMART CHOICES

Notice that the sections of the pyramid get smaller as you move toward the top. You need the most daily servings of the foods shown in the largest section. Complex carbohydrates (kar•boh•HY•drayts) are a terrific source of energy.

Many of the foods at the base of the pyramid also contain protein. The right amount of protein builds muscles and repairs tissue. But if you eat too much protein, it turns into fat. The second level from the top of the pyramid shows foods richest in protein. Which ones do you eat every day?

The very top of the pyramid shows foods that people need least but that Americans eat too much of. "Junk foods" like candy bars and ice cream provide lots of Calories but few or no nutrients, the parts of food that keep systems healthy. To eat a more healthful diet, substitute foods from lower levels of the pyramid for desserts and snacks. For example, you could eat a bowl of strawberries instead of strawberry ice cream.

YOU LOSE WITH BOOZE!

Have you ever noticed a TV commercial for beer? The scenes of good-looking people playing games like beach volleyball suggest that using alcohol makes you healthy and popular. It does not.

Alcohol slows the nervous system. It decreases muscle control, slurs speech, and blurs vision. Alcohol also makes it hard to think clearly. After two or three alcoholic drinks, people forget how to act and what to say or not to say. These are just some immediate effects of drinking alcohol. Over time alcohol can damage not only the brain but also the heart, kidneys, stomach, intestines, and liver.

Alcohol affects many parts of the body quickly because it does not have to be digested. As a person drinks, some of the alcohol is absorbed directly into the bloodstream.

Take a lesson from boys and girls like the ones you see here. To keep their systems healthy, what will they say if offered alcohol? A firm NO!

NO SMOKING

Until about 50 years ago, people didn't know how dangerous it was to smoke tobacco. Then, in 1962, the U.S. government decided to review studies comparing the deaths of smokers and nonsmokers. These studies showed that smokers died at a younger age from cancer and other causes. The final report read, "Cigarette smoking is dangerous to your health."

Tobacco contains a poisonous chemical called nicotine (NIK•uh•teen). Nicotine speeds up the central nervous system. It stresses the heart. It narrows the blood vessels, which carry blood to all parts of the body.

Then why does anyone start smoking, and why don't all smokers quit? Two strong influences on whether people start smoking are parents and friends who smoke. As for quitting, most smokers say that they would like to but it is hard because nicotine is addictive. It is easier and much more healthful to never start.

Find Out

What does a healthy human lung look like? What about a cancerous human lung? Use reference books, computers, or encyclopedias to find pictures.

Science Fun

Lichen Cures

Years ago, doctors used the lichen old-man's beard to promote hair growth on the scalps of bald men. They used dogtooth lichen, ground and mixed with red pepper, to treat rabies. They used lung lichens (lungwort or spotted lungwort) to treat lung disease.

None of these practices worked very well. Today, lichens are used more successfully to make ointments and medicines. Finnish scientists use lichens to produce an antibiotic salve for use on wounds and burns. Scientists in Germany have begun to use lichens to produce a drug for treating tuberculosis.

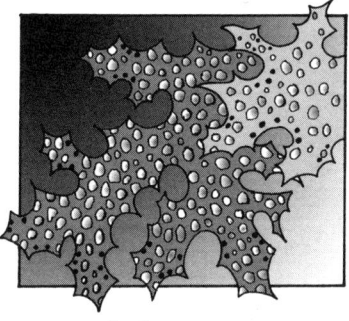

READER RIDDLES

▶ **Q:** What do you call a lichen that grows on a motorcycle?
A: *a bikin' lichen*

▶ **Q:** What do you call a lichen that plays a mean game of volleyball?
A: *a spikin' lichen*

Fold

LOOKING AT ECOSYSTEMS

Lichens

FAST FACT

There are more than 15,000 known lichen species on Earth—about 3600 of them in the United States and Canada.

FAST FACT

Most lichens grow slowly, less than 12 mm (0.5 in.) per year. Yet lichens keep growing a long time.

FAST FACT

Most lichens grow on rocks and trees. However, lichens can be found on more unusual surfaces, such as the backs of Galápagos tortoises and beetles.

LICHENS

You know about compound words like *skateboard* (*skate* + *board*) and *railroad* (*rail* + *road*). A compound word is one word made up of two words. A lichen is a compound living thing made up of two living things: a fungus and an alga.

The fungus absorbs moisture, which the alga needs. It also dissolves minerals, which nourish the lichen. The alga carries out photosynthesis. It supplies the lichen with carbohydrates.

Scientists classify lichens in three groups: crusty, leaflike, and stalked.

Crusty Lichen

◄ Crusty lichen

Crusty lichens are the smallest of the lichens. The *thallus*, or plant body, of a crusty lichen often cracks in pieces. In the Sierra Nevada mountains, bright red, yellow, and gray crusty lichens look like paint splashed on big slate slabs. Crusty lichens help protect soils from erosion in the deserts of the southwestern United States.

Vocabulary Fun

WORD SEARCH

Locate and circle the words in the puzzle below. The words can be up, down, forward, backward, or diagonal.

lichens	photosynthesis	carbohydrate
fungi	ecosystem	thallus
algae	pollution	

```
E A Q R B M S T C P D E
C F O P G K N F O H J I
O P A C H M A U T O L R
S I L I C H E N S T V E
Y R G Q A M I G S O S I
S P A P R I R I O S V E
T R E P B S C I E Y N C
E Q P O O P U L L N O N
M C T S H L Z R A T T M
H O G B Y O L S T H O P
S D O G D H I U B E Y E
L O N G R K A T T S D E
S U L L A H T V E I L O
P I N G T O X Y G S O E
N S O I E L T A P E R N
```

COLOR MAGIC

Scientists and other people use *indicators* to tell whether a solution is an acid or a base. You can use red cabbage to make an indicator.

MATERIALS

- ▶ 1 measuring cup
- ▶ 3 small glasses
- ▶ boiling water
- ▶ red cabbage leaves
- ▶ bicarbonate of soda
- ▶ 1 bowl
- ▶ white vinegar

PROCEDURE

1. Have an adult cut a red cabbage leaf into small pieces. Soak it in a cup of boiling water for half an hour. You can now use the violet-colored water for color magic.
2. Pour water into one glass. In the second glass, place white vinegar, and in the third, put water mixed with bicarbonate of soda.
3. When you pour a little cabbage water into each glass, the first liquid turns violet, the second turns red, and the third turns green. The violet cabbage dye turns red in acid and green in bases. In water it does not change color.

CONCLUSIONS

Which of the substances that you tested is an acid? Which is a base? How do you think an indicator might be useful?

Fold

LEAFLIKE LICHENS

Leaflike lichens are the easiest to recognize. They look like lacy or ruffled carpets.

Rock tripe is a leaflike lichen named by fur trappers in Canada long ago. Rock tripe contained enough starch to keep trappers from starving when they ran out of food. The recipe below tells how to prepare rock tripe. (**Don't try it at home!**)

Leaflike lichen ▲

Rock Tripe

First, gather rock tripe, and wash it as clean as possible of sand and grit. Wash it again and again, snipping off the gritty parts where the lichen held on to the rock. Then, roast it slowly in a pan, until it is dry and crisp. Next, boil it for one hour, and serve it either hot or cold.

Find Out

Native Americans have long used lichens as a source of dye. Find out how lichens are used today by Navajo weavers. Use books, computers, or encyclopedias to find information. Then make a color drawing of a Navajo rug.

STALKED LICHEN

Stalked lichens vary widely in appearance. Some, like old-man's beard, hang from trees in thin, matted strands. Others grow straight up from a base on the ground.

A stalked lichen known as reindeer moss provides food for caribou and reindeer during long, cold winters.

Some lichens live for thousands of years. This makes them some of the oldest living things on Earth. Scientists can use very old lichens to tell the age of objects from ancient civilizations and to track processes, like glacier movement, that have occurred over time.

Think & Do

Kay is a historian. She wants to find the age of a stone wall. She sees lichens that have been growing on the wall for many years. Kay measures the largest lichen on the wall. It has a circle shape with a radius of 100 millimeters. Kay knows that as this lichen species grows, it increases its radius 2 millimeters each year. To tell the lichen's age, she divides the lichen's radius by its growth per year. Help Kay by finding the quotient.

POLLUTION DETECTORS

You have learned that lichens can grow in all sorts of climates and all sorts of places. But lichens cannot survive pollution. If pollution enters the ground, lichens absorb it. If pollution enters the air, lichens absorb pollution along with the oxygen that they need.

All the parts of an ecosystem are connected. One change in an ecosystem affects the whole ecosystem. In 1986 an accident in a nuclear power plant in what is now the Ukraine formed toxic (poisonous) clouds in the atmosphere. The clouds moved over Lapland, where reindeer graze. Then the clouds fell to Earth as radioactive snow. Toxic snow fell onto reindeer moss. The reindeer moss absorbed the poison. Reindeer who grazed on reindeer moss were poisoned, too. People who usually eat reindeer had to go without meat that year, because the reindeer meat was also poisoned.

There is a bright side to stories like this one. Because lichens are so sensitive to pollution, they can be used as an early warning system. Lichens can warn people about pollution before the lichens themselves are badly harmed. Then people can take action to stop pollution.

Fold

Science Fun

Ms. Millard bought a farm where only corn was grown for many years. Her goal is to produce one money-making crop each year while conserving the nutrients in her soil.

Help Ms. Millard plan what crops to grow over the next six years. Present your plan by filling in the table at the bottom of the page. Use the pictures below and what you know about nitrogen loss and replacement as a guide. Explain your choices to a family member or friend.

Corn   Tobacco   Cotton   Ms. Millard   Soybean   Barley   Sorghum   Oats

Year Number	Crop
1	
2	
3	
4	
5	
6	

Answers to Vocabulary Fun: 1. b. intercropping, 2. c. windbreak, 3. a. no-till farming, 4. d. terracing

SOIL CONSERVATION

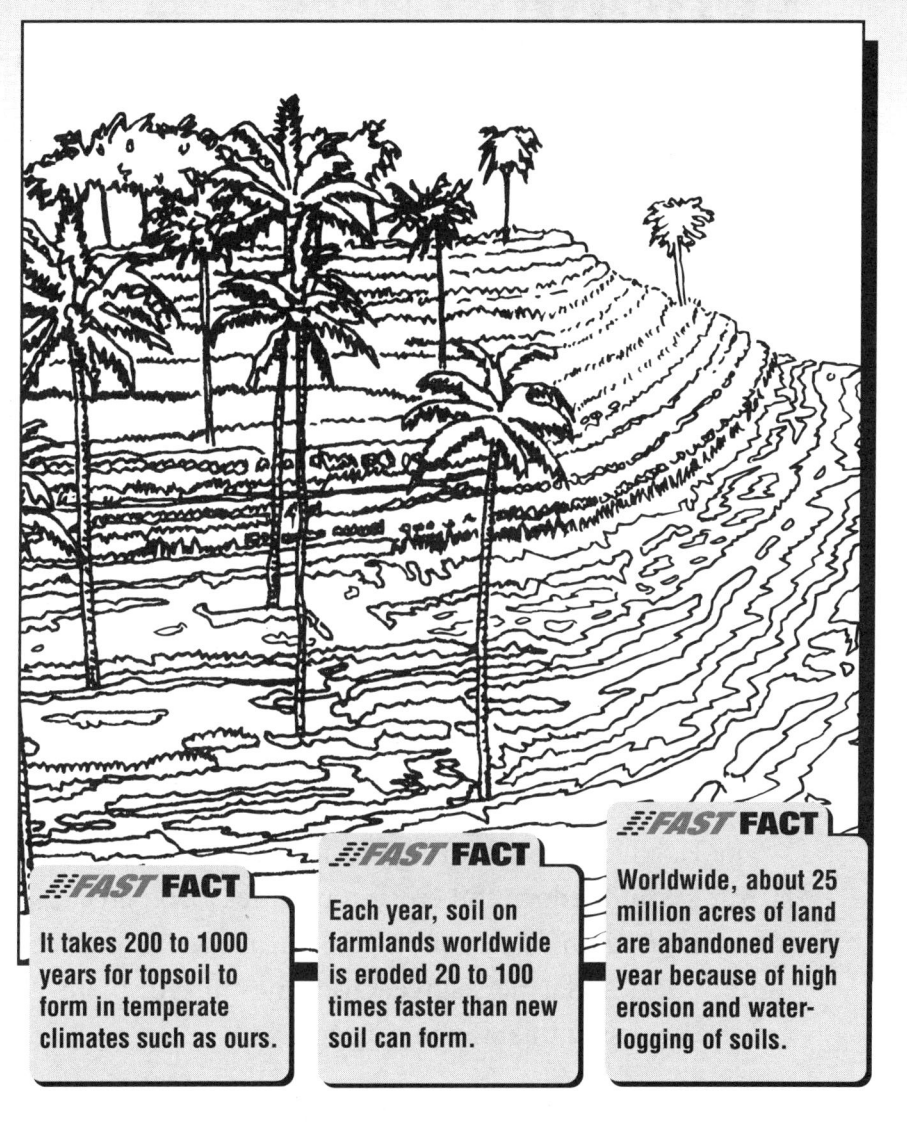

FAST FACT
It takes 200 to 1000 years for topsoil to form in temperate climates such as ours.

FAST FACT
Each year, soil on farmlands worldwide is eroded 20 to 100 times faster than new soil can form.

FAST FACT
Worldwide, about 25 million acres of land are abandoned every year because of high erosion and water-logging of soils.

SLOWING EROSION

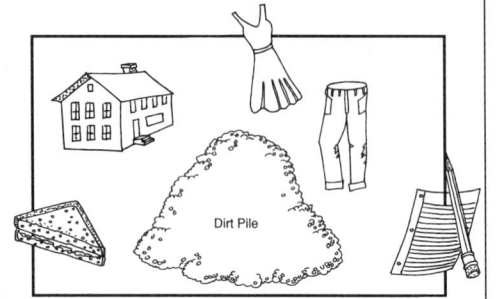

Dirt Pile

It looks like, well, dirt. Who would guess that it is one of Earth's most valuable resources? Yet most of our food, clothing, and buildings depend on soil.

You have read about some ways to protect soil. *Contour plowing* catches and slows runoff. *Strip cropping* slows wind erosion. *Terracing* increases crop-growing areas and slows water erosion.

Another technique, called *no-till farming*, is widely used on U.S. croplands. Farmers who use this technique leave the remains of their crop in the soil. This keeps the soil from being washed away. The machines they use break up subsoil without turning over topsoil. Planting machines can place seeds into slits made in unplowed soil.

The U.S. Department of Agriculture says that no-till farming could reduce soil erosion by at least 50 percent, if it were used on 80 percent of U.S. farms. More and more American farmers agree. Over one-third of them are already using this way to conserve soil.

Vocabulary Fun

Circle the letter of the best vocabulary word to complete the sentence.

1. If you are growing several crops together in one field, you are _____.
   a. interviewing
   b. intercropping
   c. crop dusting
   d. weathering

2. Rows of trees of different heights that protect fields from the wind are a conservation tool called a _____.
   a. breakdown
   b. tree farm
   c. windbreak
   d. breakfront

3. Farmers who leave the remains of their crops in the soil and use very little tilling to plant the new seeds are using a conservation method called _____.
   a. no-till farming
   b. no-fault farming
   c. till-man farming
   d. no-chance farming

4. Farming using wide, flat rows built into a hillside is known as _____.
   a. bordering
   b. fertilizing
   c. erosion
   d. terracing

Answers on page 8

FROM MEALS TO MULCH

Do this activity to see how leftovers can decompose to enrich soil.

MATERIALS

▶ **pencil and paper** ▶ **apple core**

▶ **spade or shovel** ▶ **meterstick**

▶ **several rocks** ▶ **pair of work gloves**

PROCEDURE

1. Draw the apple core. Label the drawing *Before*. Save your drawing. Ask an adult for permission to dig a hole in your backyard or another area. Dig one hole, about 6 inches deep and a little wider than the apple core. Wear gloves. Place the apple core in the hole. Refill the hole with soil. Use the rocks to mark the spot.
2. After one month, dig up the apple core. (Remember to wear the gloves.) Observe the piece of apple. Draw a picture of what you see now. Label it *After*.

CONCLUSIONS

What happened to the apple core? The apple core is biodegradable. That means it can become part of the soil again. As the core rots, it provides a home for microorganisms that help release nutrients into the soil. How do you think the apple core affected the soil?

Fold

KEEPING SOIL FERTILE

Erosion is not the only threat to healthy soil. Farmers must also work to keep soil fertile. One way is crop rotation. Farmers have used this technique all over the world for hundreds of years.

Intercropping is another old way of controlling nutrient loss in soil. Intercropping is growing several crops together in one field. Before Europeans arrived in what are now Canada and the United States, Native Americans planted together crops that they called the three sisters—squash, corn, and beans. The bean vines were supported by the tall corn stalks. The squash crept between the corn and beans. Squash shaded out weeds and helped enrich the soil. After the beans were harvested, Native Americans turned the bean plants back into the soil. Do you recall how beans help soil? (by adding nitrogen)

Suppose you are a farmer who plows your land each year. Someone suggests that you try no-till farming. What questions would you ask before changing the way you grow crops? Write your questions. Share them with a family member.

SOIL CONSERVATION AROUND THE WORLD

All over the world, people work to conserve soil. The drawings on these two pages show some ways people have been successful.

Planting trees helps prevent erosion by wind and rain. This orchard of fruit trees was planted in eastern China on what was once a bare hill.

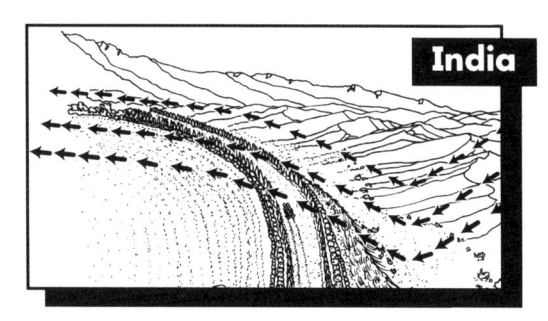

People in India plant windbreaks like these to reduce erosion on farm fields. The windbreaks are rows made up of one tall tree, one shorter tree, and one small shrub. By using plants of different heights, people can direct wind currents in a way that conserves soil.

This picture shows how people in Peru use intercropping, as did Native Americans long ago. Peruvian farmers plant several crops together in strips between trees and shrubs. The trees help keep soil in place and give shade. The shade slows evaporation and helps the soil retain moisture.

An Illinois farmer uses two techniques—contour planting and intercropping—to reduce erosion on gently sloping land.

Find Out

How do farmers or gardeners conserve soil in the area where you live? To find information, use newspaper articles, local library resources, or conversations with gardeners you know. Draw a picture with captions to show what you find.

Fold

Science Fun

Over Hill, Over Dale on the Appalachian Trail

The Appalachian Trail (AT) runs from Springer Mountain, in Georgia, to Mount Katahdin, in Maine. Each year about 200 "thru-hikers," some of them in their seventies, hike the whole 3435-km (2135-mi) trail. Many hikers travel using nicknames such as Hikin' Barbarian or Spirit Walker.

Emma "Grandma" Gatewood finished her second thru-hike of the Appalachian Trail a few days before she turned 70 years old.

READER RIDDLES

▶ **Q:** Where do people on the Capital Area Greenway often find themselves?

A: *(up the creek)*

▶ **Q:** Where did the principal send the lizard that misbehaved?

A: *(to the wildlife corridor)*

Answers to Vocabulary Fun: Hidden message: Conservation protects ecosystems.

PROTECTING ECOSYSTEMS

Greenways

Fold

FAST FACT

The first greenway was built in 1865 in California. It was built to enable people to drive or walk to a scenic overlook of a nearby canyon.

FAST FACT

Approximately 80 percent of Americans live and work in cities or suburbs. Greenways offer them and their children a chance to experience wildlife.

FAST FACT

Since its founding in 1986, Rails-to-Trails Conservancy has helped make more than 9654 km (about 6000 mi) of bike paths in 44 states.

GREENWAYS

Do you and your friends ride bicycles on a path that links one park to another? Do you in-line skate on a paved trail with streams or woods on either side? If so, you may be using a *greenway*. A greenway is a path through an open area that people use for recreational activities.

Wheelchair users, bicyclists, and joggers on a greenway in Augusta, Georgia.

Greenways may be very short or miles long. They may be paved roads or dirt paths. Some greenways cross state lines. Some greenways link communities within cities like San Francisco and Boston. What greenways have in common is preservation. They preserve green space from building development. Greenways help preserve habitat for plants. They provide wildlife corridors, routes that wild animals can use to move safely through urban areas.

Vocabulary Fun

Hidden Message

Write the missing letters in the sentences.

1. G__ee__w__ys preser__e wildlife.
    5   3   8   7

2. Pe__ple need to __r__serve ecos__stems.
    2   11 6   12

3. A bike pa__h helps __onservation efforts.
            9   1

4. Wildl__fe corridor__ provide wild ani__als a safe
    10   4   13
route through urban areas.

Below, write the letters on the line that matches the numbers. Read the hidden message.

__	__	__	__	__	__	__	__	__	__	__	__
1	2	3	4	6	5	7	8	9	10	2	2

__	__	__	__	__	__	__	__
11	5	2	9	6	1	9	4

__	__	__	__	__	__	__	__	__	__
6	1	2	4	12	4	9	6	13	4

PLAN A GREENWAY

Do this activity to explore how a greenway could be built, or an existing greenway could be improved near you.

MATERIALS

► **map of your city, town, or nearest town**
► **colored marker** ► **pencil**

PROCEDURE

1. Study the map. Look for an area that could be set aside as a greenway. Use the pencil to sketch your greenway on the map. (Or copy a portion of the map on a separate sheet of paper, and sketch the greenway on your copy.) When you have the greenway as you want it, use the marker to make it stand out.

2. You may wish to add plants on the borders of your greenway or to add side paths to nearby waterways if your greenway lies along a stream, lake, or river.

CONCLUSIONS

What natural features would your greenway preserve? What places would it allow people to reach without driving? What animals might use your greenway as a corridor?

Fold

A GREENWAY WITH A VIEW

A greenway can be an open outdoor space. It can be a natural or landscaped path. Some greenways are bicycle paths. Some greenways are roads for motor vehicles laid out along preserved wildlands. A *viewshed* is the scenery that can be seen from a greenway or park.

The Big Sur viewshed preserves more than 161 km (about 100 mi.) of wilderness along a California state highway. For plants and animals, the Big Sur viewshed provides protected habitat. For people, it offers a beautiful drive.

Driving along the Big Sur viewshed, you can see giant redwood trees and mountain streams that flow into the Pacific Ocean. You can see seals sunning themselves on small rock islands. Eyesores such as billboards have been banned by law to preserve this magnificent stretch of California coast.

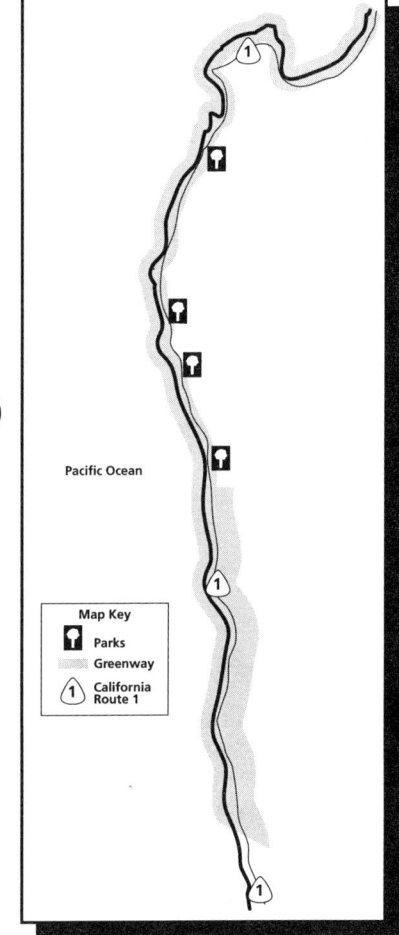

Pacific Ocean

Map Key
🚹 Parks
▨ Greenway
① California Route 1

THE GREENWAY DADDY

Bill Flournoy is known as the "father of the Raleigh greenways." It all began for Flournoy in 1970. Flournoy wanted Raleigh, North Carolina, to remain the lovely, green city that he knew growing up. So Flournoy outlined a plan for a network of greenways through all the neighborhoods in Raleigh.

Raleigh's leaders approved Flournoy's idea for a greenway program. In 1974, they started to work. People came from other cities to observe the growing greenway system. Over time, the Capital Area Greenway became the model for more than 35 other greenways in North Carolina.

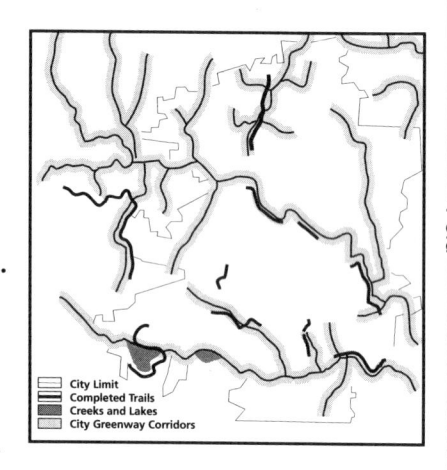

City Limit
Completed Trails
Creeks and Lakes
City Greenway Corridors

Suppose you lived near an old railroad bed that some people thought would make a great bicycle trail. How would you and your family feel about the idea? Make a list of questions that you would ask and suggestions you would make.

ON THE PATH

The students of Mr. Levy's fourth grade class in Lexington, Massachusetts, wrote a book called *On the Path*. The book tells about a bike path that runs through their community.

The students studied the bike path thoroughly. They went to Lexington's Town Hall and spoke with town leaders to find information. They rode the 11-mile bike path from one end to the other. These are some of the things that they found out.

The bikeway took two years to build. It took fifteen years to plan.	
The bike path is bordered by wetlands.	
Some funding for the bikeway came from the federal Clean Air Act.	
The town of Lexington planted rye grass along the bike path to stop erosion.	
From the bike path people have seen many wild animals.	

Science Fun

POCKET GOPHER TO THE RESCUE!

This small furry creature about the size of a hamster doesn't look like a hero. Before the explosion, it was best known for making gopher burrows in people's carefully tended lawns. But the northern pocket gopher acted as a hero after the explosion of Mount St. Helens.

Many pocket gophers, safe in their burrows, survived the blast. As they burrowed through the ash, they mixed ash with the rich soil.

Seeds carried by the wind fell on the soil the pocket gophers pushed up. The seeds grew into plants. The plants attracted insects, which attracted birds. Then other mammals, like the squirrel and elk, came into the blast zone, hunting for food. The cycle of life had begun again.

Answers to Vocabulary Fun: 1. lava, 2. Mount St. Helens, 3. magma, 4. Washington, 5. volcano

Fold

VOLCANOES

Mount St. Helens

FAST FACT
On May 18, 1980, Mount St. Helens in the state of Washington erupted with the force of a 30-megaton bomb.

FAST FACT
Before the eruption blew the top off Mount St. Helens, it was Washington's fifth-highest peak, at 2950 m (about 9677 ft).

FAST FACT
The entire north half of Mount St. Helens slid downhill in the explosion, causing the largest avalanche in recorded history.

THE EXPLOSION

The drawing on page 1 shows Mount St. Helens before the 1980 eruption. It was a cone with smooth sides, a pointed crest, and a year-round cap of snow.

But it was also a composite volcano. For 123 years, Mount St. Helens had been dormant, or sleeping. In the spring of 1980, it began to awaken. These drawings show what happened next.

Original Shape of Mountain; Magma

1. Magma rising from deep inside the mountain pushed a bulge outward from its northern slope.

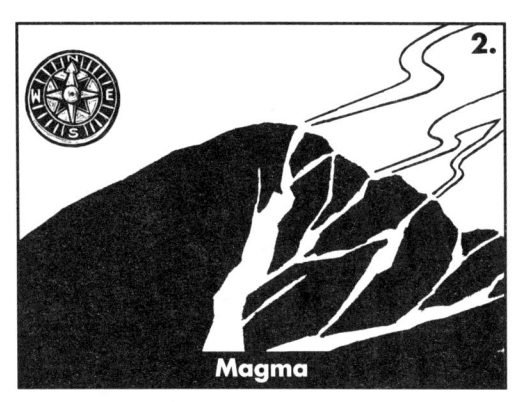

Magma

2. An earthquake shook the bulge loose. The earthquake caused an avalanche. The avalanche released great pressure that held the magma and gases inside the volcano. The volcano erupted northward, blowing off the top of Mount St. Helens.

VocabularyFun

RIDDLES

WHAT AM I?

1. I am the hot melted rock flowing out of a volcano. What am I?

   _____

2. I am the mountain that exploded in 1980. What am I?

   _____

3. I am the melted rock inside the Earth. What am I?

   _____

4. I am the state where Mount St. Helens is located. What am I?

   _____

5. I formed when melted rock and gases erupted from a hole in the Earth's surface. What am I?

   _____

Answers on page 8

UNDERWATER VOLCANO

Do this activity to model volcanic activity on the ocean floor.

MATERIALS

- ▶ piece of string
- ▶ large, clear bowl
- ▶ cold and hot tap water
- ▶ food coloring
- ▶ small, clear glass bottle

PROCEDURE

1. Use cold water. Fill the bowl about $\frac{3}{4}$ full. Tie the string firmly around the bottle neck. Squeeze 5 to 10 drops of food coloring into the bottle. Then have an adult fill the bottle with hot water from the faucet. **CAUTION: Be careful with the hot water.**

2. Lift the bottle by the string. Gently lower the bottle so that it is lying on its side on the bottom of the bowl. Observe what happens.

CONCLUSIONS

What acted as hot lava and gases from a deep sea vent? What allowed you to see the movement of the eruption?

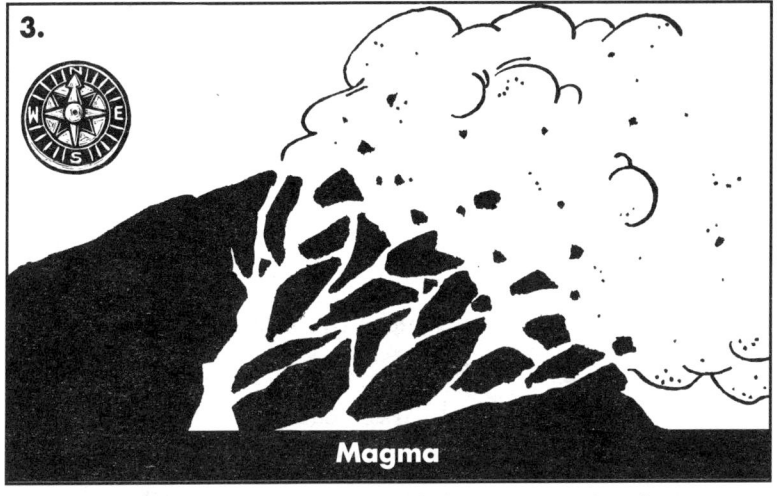

3.

Magma

3. Having blown off the top of the mountain, the erupting column of gases, ash, and lava went straight up. It was propelled by a chain reaction of explosions that moved down into the mountain's core.

Think & Do

Predict what will happen if you shake a sealed carbonated drink (like cola) and quickly open it. Test your prediction. Work outdoors or in a sink. CAUTION: Wear safety goggles. Do this activity only with an adult partner. Clean up after you are through.

You modeled an erupting volcano. With your partner's help, explain how. What acted as magma? How did you cause pressure to build up in the "volcano"?

THE UNDERLYING CAUSE

Some volcanoes form where plates move toward each other. Not far from Mount St. Helens, about 100 miles off the Northwest coast, lies a small, expanding plate known as the Juan de Fuca plate. This plate is moving toward the North American plate—which is located even closer to the mountain. Where the two plates meet, the

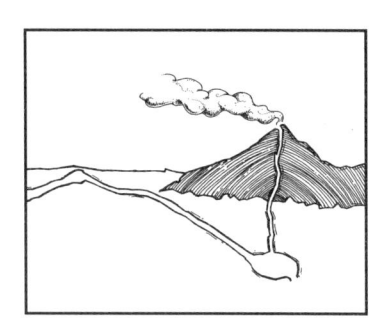

Juan de Fuca plate dives below the North American plate. When it reaches a depth of about 160 kilometers (100 mi), the Juan de Fuca plate begins to melt. Magma and gases from the melting plate blasted out in the eruption of Mount St. Helens.

Volcanic eruptions cause rapid changes on Earth. When Mount St. Helens erupted, every plant on the mountain was either burned or ripped off the surface. Trees blew down like matchsticks. Clear mountain lakes became tea-colored swamps. Millions of fish, birds, deer, and elk were killed.

Seventy percent of the ice and snow on Mount St. Helens melted into hot water, which caused tremendous floods. Mud surging down the mountain clogged three rivers. Ships couldn't move. Thirty-one vessels were stranded in three port cities.

SPIRIT RETURNS

Spirit Lake lies at the base of Mount St. Helens. Before the eruption, it was a crystal-clear lake whose blue-green waters reflected an upside-down image of the mountain. When Mount St. Helens blew apart, the record-breaking avalanche tumbled through Spirit Lake. Water splashed out of the lake in a wave 245 m (about 800 ft) high. One forest worker described the event as "what would happen if you ran down the hall and leaped into a full bathtub."

When the water fell back down, it deposited everything it carried—dirt, animal carcasses, trees, and rocks—into the lake. Superheated gases and rock also polluted the water. All the oxygen in the water was used up. All the fish in Spirit Lake, along with their food chain and habitat, were destroyed.

But the lake made a comeback! Ten years after the eruption, oxygen levels had returned to normal. Frogs and toads found habitats at the recovering lake. The water was healthy enough to support populations of fish.

Science Fun

Cave Animals

Animals that live in caves have adapted to conditions there. Over time, many species of cave animals have lost their sight and their coloring, and have developed long limbs and highly sensitive organs of touch.

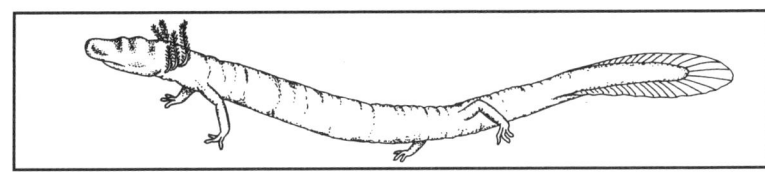

▲ The Texas blind salamander is about 10 centimeters (4 in.) long. Sensory organs along its side and head allow the salamander to locate prey.

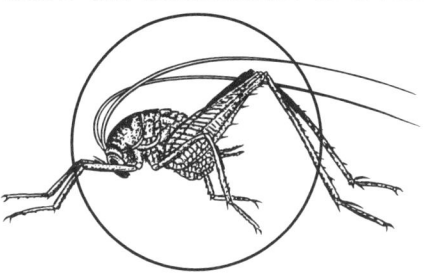

◄ The cave cricket's antennae are twice as long as those of crickets who live above ground. Above-ground crickets chirrup. The cave cricket is silent.

Most spiders that live above ► ground deposit their eggs. The cave spider carries her eggs on her back. It is too dangerous to leave the eggs unguarded.

Answers to Vocabulary Fun: 1. stalagmite, 2. cavern, 3. calcite, 4. speleothems, 5. stalactite, 6. cave rafts

---

MINERALS AND ROCKS

Limestone Caves

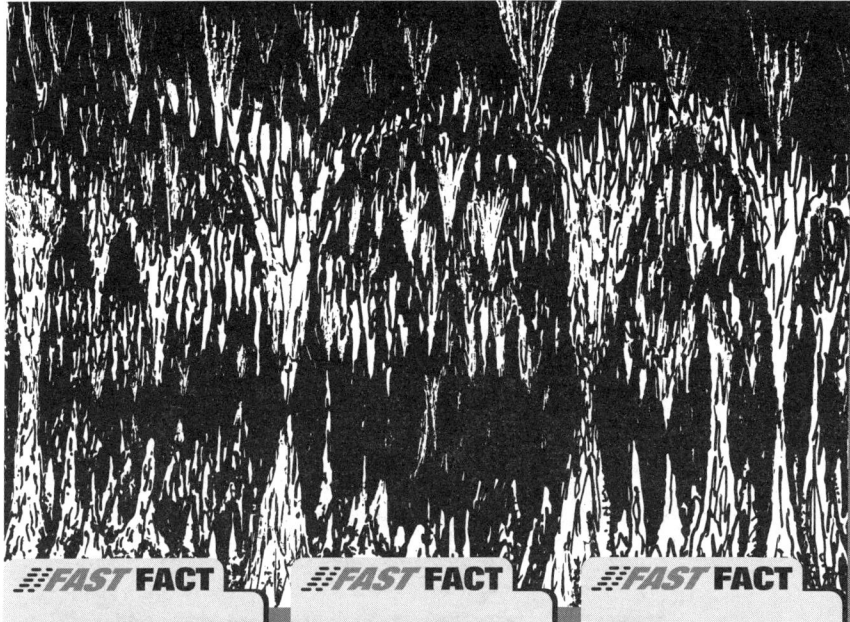

FAST FACT

The endless dripping of water in caves causes fabulous formations. The minerals dissolved in the water turn them many different beautiful colors.

FAST FACT

Cave formations can grow up to $2\frac{1}{2}$ mm (about $\frac{1}{10}$ in.) per year in some caves.

FAST FACT

People have given many cave formations funny names, like "Fatman's Misery" or "King's Bed Chamber."

Fold

LIMESTONE CAVES

Limestone caves form underground in areas where there is a lot of limestone. Caves are cool and dark. Green plants can't live in them because there is no light for photosynthesis.

Animals that live in caves have adapted to the darkness. (Turn to page 8 to see some cave-dwelling animals.) The drawing below and the one on page 3 show the stages of development of a limestone cave.

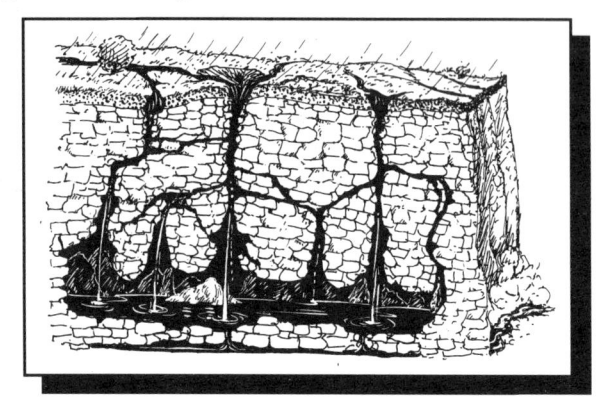

You can summarize cave development in one word: erosion. Water from rain, streams, or rivers seeps down through tiny cracks in the limestone. The water becomes acidic as it flows through decaying plants and animals. The acidic water slowly dissolves the limestone and makes the cracks larger.

VocabularyFun

CRYPTOGRAM

Use the code to write the secret words.

A-1	E-5	I-9	M-13	Q-17	U-21	Y-25
B-2	F-6	J-10	N-14	R-18	V-22	Z-26
C-3	G-7	K-11	O-15	S-19	W-23	
D-4	H-8	L-12	P-16	T-20	X-24	

1. __ __ __ __ __ __ __ __ __ __
   19 20 1 12 1 7 13 9 20 5

2. __ __ __ __ __ __
   3 1 22 5 18 14

3. __ __ __ __ __ __ __
   3 1 12 3 9 20 5

4. __ __ __ __ __ __ __ __ __ __ __
   19 16 5 12 5 15 20 8 5 13 19

5. __ __ __ __ __ __ __ __ __ __
   19 20 1 12 1 3 20 9 20 5

6. __ __ __ __ __ __ __ __ __
   3 1 22 5   18 1 6 20 19

Answers on page 8

MAKE YOUR OWN COLUMN

Do this activity to see for yourself how stalactites and stalagmites form and meet.

MATERIALS

- ▶ baking soda
- ▶ warm water
- ▶ 2 clear glass jars
- ▶ string of wool yarn or thin piece of wool
- ▶ spoon
- ▶ saucer
- ▶ 2 paper clips

PROCEDURE

Attach one paper clip to each end of the string. Fill the two jars with warm water. Spoon baking soda into the jars. Stir. Keep adding baking soda and stirring until no more dissolves. Then lower one end of the yarn into one jar. Lower the other end of the yarn into the other jar. Make sure the string is in the water in both jars. Place the saucer between the jars. Observe the setup for several days.

CONCLUSIONS

How did the solution move from the jars onto the saucer? What acted as calcite in your model? Think about how real stalactites and stalagmites are made. What is needed to make these cave formations?

UNDERGROUND FORMATIONS

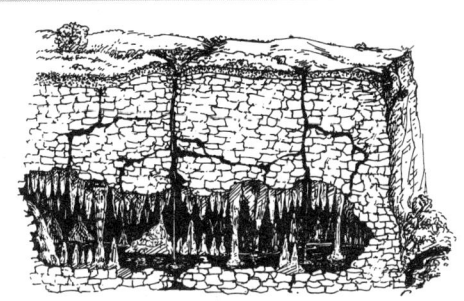

Water dissolves more and more limestone. Over time, an underground chamber forms. The process may repeat many times. Water dissolves more limestone to form new cave passages and chambers at lower levels.

Calcite Sculptures

Limestone is a fine-grained sedimentary rock. It is made up mostly of the mineral calcite. Stalactites and stalagmites are made of calcite, too. As water drips down from the limestone ceiling of a cave, it leaves calcite deposits behind. Often, the deposits thicken into stalactites that point down toward the cave floor. Meanwhile, water that drips onto the cave floor forms stalagmites that point up. Stalactites and stalagmites grow slowly, about $2\frac{1}{2}$ millimeters ($\frac{1}{10}$ in.) in one year.

Find Out

Find information about Carlsbad Caverns National Park in New Mexico or Mammoth Cave National Park in Kentucky. Find out when and how the cave was first explored. Use travel guides, books, or encyclopedias.

Fold

WATER THE SHAPER

Water is the shaper of caves. Water leaves behind different speleothems (SPEE•lee•uh•themz), or cave formations, depending on how it drips or flows and what minerals it contains. You have learned about two speleothems, stalactites and stalagmites. The drawing below shows some of the many others.

Water dripping from the ceiling forms tiny tubes of calcite known as *soda straws*. If a tube remains unblocked, the soda straw stays thin and grows longer. If a tube gets blocked, water flows down the outside. Slowly, the soda straw thickens into a stalactite.

Water trickling along the slanted ceiling of a cave deposits winding trails of calcite known as *cave draperies*, or curtains.

Water that seeps into the cave from tiny cracks in the limestone makes delicate, curving speleothems known as *helictites*.

Thin, round patches of calcite form floating *cave rafts* on underground pools.

Flat deposits of calcite known as *shelfstone* build up at the edges of cave pools. Shelfstone also forms on columns that stand in water. If the pool drains away, the shelfstone remains.

Calcite can build up around tiny particles in a shallow cave pool. Constantly dripping water bounces and rounds the particles into *cave pearls*.

Use what you learned in this article to make a limestone cave. Draw the cave or construct it using modeling clay. Share your model with classmates.

Science Fun

Name That Fossil

Each type of fossil below has been found in the Petrified Forest. Label each fossil as a trace fossil, carbon film, or petrified fossil.

READER RIDDLES

▶ **Q:** What do you call a frightened fossil?

   A: *Petrified.*

▶ **Q:** What is the favorite music of all petrified logs?

   A: *Rock and roll.*

▶ **Q:** What do you call a traffic accident in the Petrified Forest?

   A: *A log jam.*

Answers to Vocabulary Fun: 1. petrify, 2. silicon, 3. fossil, 4. crystal, 5. forest
Name that fossil: petrified fossil; carbon film, trace fossil

FOSSILS

The Petrified Forest

FAST FACT

Petrified wood is heavy. One cubic foot of it weighs about 745 N (about 168 lb).

FAST FACT

The petrified forest was buried for almost 200 million years. Then wind and water began slowly carrying away soil that covered the logs.

FAST FACT

Large cavities, or hollow places, within the logs of the petrified forest are sometimes lined with crystals of gemstones like rose or smoky quartz and amethyst.

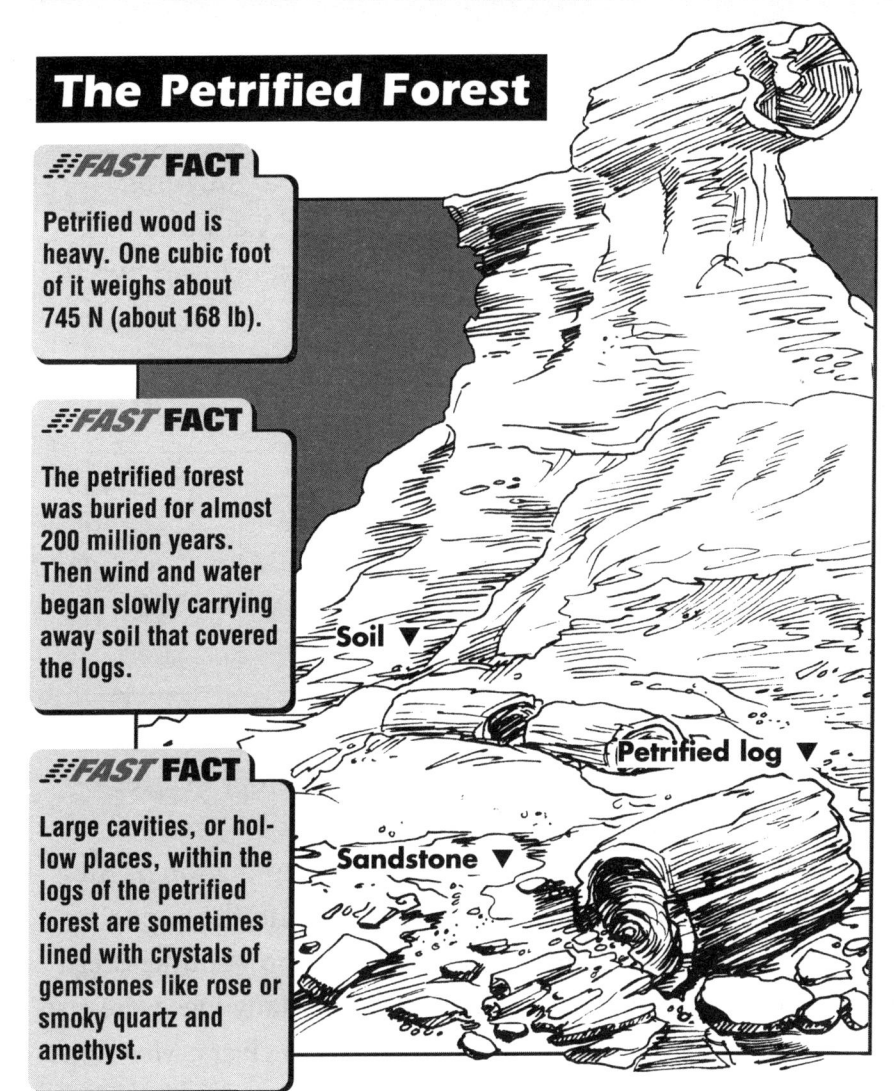

Soil ▼

Petrified log ▼

Sandstone ▼

Fold

PETRIFIED FOREST
Geologic History

The geologic time scale is divided into four eras: Precambrian, Paleozoic, Mesozoic, and Cenozoic. The eras are divided into periods. The chart below shows the periods of the Mesozoic Era, when the Petrified Forest was formed. Most of the rocks in the forest were deposited early in the era, during the Triassic Period.

Era	Period	M.Y.B.P.
M E S O Z O I C	Cretaceous	136
	Jurassic	190
	Triassic	225

The composition of rocks, soils, and sand (what they are made of) helps tell the geologic history of a region. Look at the drawing of a pedestal rock on page 1. Sandstone and petrified wood make up the top of the pedestal. The sandstone was carried into the region by streams from mountains in what are now southeastern Arizona and southern New Mexico. Many logs were also carried into the region by streams and rivers. Most logs decay over time. These logs did not.

VocabularyFun
Rebus Vocabulary

See if you can solve the puzzles and guess the vocabulary word for which each stands.

crystal	fossil
silicon	forest
petrify	

1.  +  +

_____ + _____ + _____ = _____

2.

_____ + _____ = _____

3. f + _____ − t + _____ = _____

4.

_____ + _____ = _____

5.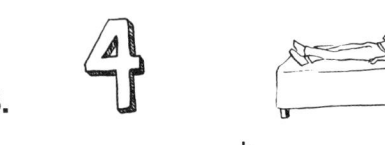

_____ + _____ = _____

Answers on page 8

Fold

HOW DO FOSSILS FORM?

Many plant fossils in the Petrified Forest are carbon films of leaves, stems, seeds, and cones. Do this activity to learn something about what a carbon film looks like and how it forms.

MATERIALS

▶ leaf
▶ $\frac{3}{4}$ cup water
▶ $\frac{1}{2}$ cup salt
▶ rolling pin
▶ sheet of wax paper
▶ 2 cups flour
▶ clock, watch, or timer

PROCEDURE

1. Mix the flour and salt. Add the water to make dough.
2. Knead the dough for about five minutes.
3. Break off a chunk of dough. Place it on the wax paper. Use the rolling pin to smooth it. Press the leaf carefully and firmly into the rolled-out dough. Carefully remove the leaf. Let the dough sit for one or two days.

CONCLUSIONS

In what ways is your fossil like a carbon film of a leaf? In what ways is it different? Think about how real fossils are made. Why are large amounts of time necessary to make all real fossils?

FOSSILS FORM

Instead they formed tree fossils. The streams that carried the logs contained an element called silicon. The silicon-rich water soaked through the logs. Then silicon combined with oxygen to form crystals of the mineral quartz. Over time, quartz crystals replaced the soft parts of the fallen trees. The wood was changed to stone.

The water contained other elements besides silicon. These elements added colors to the white or gray of the quartz. Manganese added black and sometimes pink to the petrifying wood. Iron produced mostly yellows, reds, and browns. Rarely, cobalt and chromium produced blue and green. Often the colors blended to produce a range of color tones.

Think & Do

Color this cross-section of petrified wood. Use what you learned on this page to color your drawing. Make a key that shows the elements that produced each color.

Fold

FOSSIL CLUES

Some of the animals in the Triassic looked like crocodiles today. Many _phytosaur_ (FYT•uh•sawr) fossils have been found in the park. The location of their nostrils, on a hump between and in front of their eyes, shows that phytosaurs could probably stay hidden for a long time under water while hunting prey.

Petrified bones, teeth, and other animal parts have also been found in the Petrified Forest. They, along with several other types of plant and animal fossils, give clues about what life was like there in late Triassic times.

Coelophysis (see•loh•FY•sis) was one of the earliest known dinosaurs in the Petrified Forest region. It was a small dinosaur—only about 2.4 meters (8 ft) long with a weight of 22.7 kilograms (50 lbs).

Most of the petrified logs came from cone-bearing trees. Some trees grew up to 60 meters (200 ft) tall.

Find Out

More than 300 Indian ruins are located in Petrified Forest National Park. Use reference books, travel guides, National Park Service publications, or encyclopedias to find information about one of these sites. Possibilities include Flattop Village, Twin Butte Village, and the Puerco Indian Ruin. Share your findings with classmates.

Science Fun

Riding the Air Waves

Gliders are lightweight motorless planes. They are towed into the sky by an airplane. Then they drop the tow rope and soar on the winds. A steady wind blowing against a mountain ridge will lift the glider and carry it long distances. Waves of wind coming off a mountain-top—like water flowing over a rock—also help gliders rise. Glider pilots try to locate areas of *thermal lift,* caused by uneven heating of the Earth. On the rising air waves, gliders can fly as high as 12,200 meters (about 40,000 ft) and as far as 1600 kilometers (about 1000 mi).

WIND WIT

▶ **Q:** When will it rain in India?
  A: *"Hey, man—soon!"*

▶ **Q:** Why did the kite want to fly?
  A: *It was an uplifting experience.*

Answers to Vocabulary Fun: 1. sea, 2. chinook, 3. local, 4. wind, 5. valley, 6. prevailing, 7. mountain, 8. breeze, 9. air, 10. monsoon. Hidden message: snow eaters

WIND

Fold

FAST FACT
Chinook winds have been known to raise temperatures as much as 25°C (about 45°F) in three hours.

FAST FACT
The highest wind speed ever recorded was 370 km (about 230 mi) per hour at Mt. Washington Observatory in New Hampshire.

FAST FACT
"Waves" of wind blowing off mountain-tops can reach as high as 24 km (about 15 mi) into the atmosphere.

WIND

Wind can lift the hat off your head or blow down a house. It can suddenly warm a cold winter day, or blow cool refreshing air over a hot, sunny beach. Wind is a very important part of our weather. The movement of air we call wind is caused by uneven heating of the Earth's atmosphere.

Some winds blow over large areas of the Earth, almost always in the same direction. These are called *prevailing winds*. They are caused by the sun and the Earth's rotation. Other winds, which blow over smaller, more limited areas, are called *local winds*. They are caused by land and water formations nearby.

Vocabulary Fun

Fill out the grid using the clues below. Then read down the vertical rows. One will spell out the nickname for one kind of wind.

1.
2.
3.
4.
5.
6.
7.
8.
9.
10.

1. breeze moving inland off the water

2. warm mountain winds common in the western United States

3. winds located in your area

4. movement of air

5. breeze moving up the mountainside

6. winds that blow over large areas of Earth

7. breeze coming down slopes into a valley

8. gentle movement of air

9. movement of this causes wind

10. tropical sea breeze carrying heavy rains

HIDDEN MESSAGE: _____

Answers on page 8

Fold

MAKE A MICROWIND DETECTOR

Winds can be large or small. Tiny amounts of moving air are called microwinds.

MATERIALS

▶ **pencil**

▶ **tape**

▶ **tissue**

PROCEDURE

1. Use the tape to attach one corner of the tissue to the pencil. Blow gently on the tissue to make sure it can move freely. This is your microwind detector.
2. Hold your microwind detector next to the bottom of a window or door. If the tissue moves, is the air that is moving it warm or cold?
3. Hold the microwind detector above a light bulb that has been on for a few minutes. Does the tissue move?
4. Look for microwinds in many different locations in your home. Make a chart naming each location and the results you get there.

CONCLUSIONS

Did you find any microwinds in your house? What do you think caused the winds? What does this tell you about the movement of air?

BREEZES

Mountains and valleys can cause some kinds of local winds. During the day, the sun warms the mountain slopes and the air next to the slopes. Cooler valley air then moves up the mountainside, pushing the lighter warm air up. This is called a *valley breeze*. After the slopes cool down in the evening, the colder air, which is heavier than the warm air, slides down into the valleys. That is why, if you are camped in a valley, you might feel a cold *mountain breeze* coming down the slopes as you crawl into your tent for the night.

Sea and land breezes are two other kinds of local winds. During the day, land heats up faster than water. The warm air above the land is lighter than the cool air over the sea. The cool *sea breeze* blows in to push the warm air up  and replace it. At night the land cools more quickly than the water. This causes a cool *land breeze* to blow out to sea, pushing up the warm air there and replacing it.

Fold

CHINOOKS

Chinooks are a kind of warm mountain wind. They are named after the Chinook Indians in Oregon, who called these warm winds "snow eaters." Not only do Chinooks "eat snow," they also raise temperatures 10°C to 45°C (about 20°F to 80°F) during cold winter days. Once, in 1943, a Chinook warmed the town of Spearfish, South Dakota, from -20°C to 4°C (about -4°F to 40°F) in just two minutes!

Chinooks form when mild, moist air from the Pacific coast strikes mountain ranges running north and south. The mild western winds push up over the tops of the mountains. Water vapor in the winds cools and condenses, which releases heat into the air as it drops down over the mountains.

Think & Do

Look up northers, the Santa Anas, the Mistral, the Bora, the Sirocco, and the Foehn in references and use a world map to show where these winds are located.

MONSOONS

Monsoons are a kind of giant sea breeze. They occur from April through October when the sun beats down on the land in southern and southeastern Asia. The hot air above the land is pushed up by a southwesterly wind from the Indian Ocean that carries warm, moist air over the land. Water vapor in the hot air condenses and forms clouds, which send down heavy rains. The monsoons are very important to the farmers in the countries of India, Thailand, and other parts of southern Asia. If the monsoons fail to bring the needed rain, crops may wither and livestock die. But very heavy monsoon rains can also destroy crops and homes. One severe monsoon in India dropped 5 meters (about 16 ft) of rain in fifteen days!

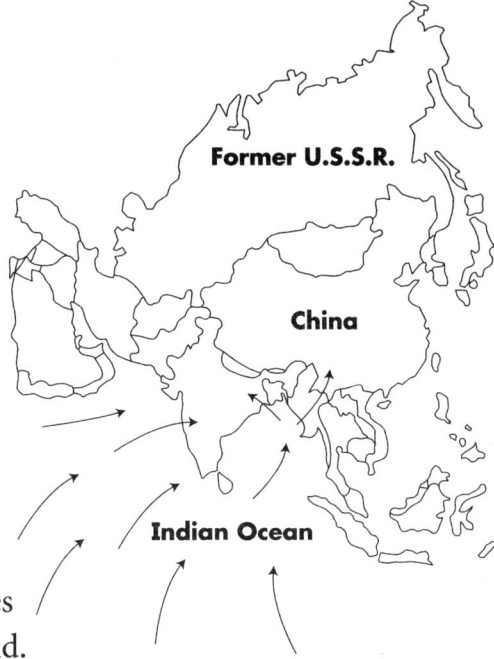

Former U.S.S.R.

China

Indian Ocean

Find Out

Use encyclopedias or other reference materials to find out about *wind shears*. What are they and what causes them? Why must pilots be especially cautious of them?

Science Fun

Amazing Creatures

Giant tube worms live near hot-water vents in the ocean floor. These strange animals have no mouths or stomachs. Instead of eating, they remove sulfur from the hot water and supply it to bacteria that live inside their bodies. The bacteria use the sulfur to make food and energy for themselves and the worms!

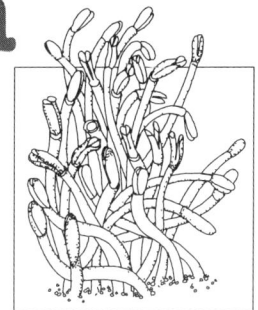

NAME THAT SUBMERSIBLE

Solve this puzzle to discover the names of three submersibles.

The first letter is J. Count five letters ahead from J. Write that letter in the second blank. Then count three letters back to find the next letter. Repeat counting five ahead and three back to fill in the blanks in order below.

J M S T N A L O R G A O R I O A E G

__ __ __ __ __ A ROBOT WITH TV CAMERAS

__ __ __ __ __ A SONAR DEVICE

__ __ __ __ CAMERA SLED OPERATED BY REMOTE CONTROL

MAPPING THE OCEAN FLOOR

▰▰FAST FACT

Millions of years ago the Mediterranean Sea was cut off from the Atlantic Ocean. The seabed rocks show that the sea has flooded and dried up many times.

▰▰FAST FACT

The average ocean depth is 3730 m (about 12,237 ft).

▰▰FAST FACT

The oceans of the world cover about 362,600,000 square km (about 140,000,000 sq mi), which is more than 70 percent of the Earth's surface.

Fold

MAPPING THE OCEAN FLOOR

Far below the surface of the oceans lie strange hidden lands. These lands have higher mountains ranges and deeper canyons than the lands above water. In deep *trenches*, or cracks, in the ocean bottom live weird sea creatures. In some places hot water spouts into the cold ocean from *vents*, or volcanic openings, in the ocean floor.

Many of these strange places are thousands of feet below the water surface where it is dark and bitterly cold. The water pressure at these depths can be several tons per square inch. No human can survive there.

But ocean scientists called *oceanographers* have discovered some amazing ways to explore these sea frontiers. They can measure depths far below those to which humans can safely travel and can produce detailed maps of the ocean floor.

Vocabulary Fun

CLUES

ACROSS

4. scientist who studies the ocean

5. deep crack in the ocean floor

6. underwater vehicle that can carry people and equipment

9. animals that live near ocean vents

DOWN

1. special submersible that can travel to great depths

2. salinity of the ocean is due to

3. volcanic opening in the ocean floor

7. bouncing sound off an object

8. another name for echo sounding

Answers on page 8

HOW SOUND TRAVELS IN WATER

As you have read, oceanographers use sound to measure ocean depths. Sound travels much faster in water than in air.

MATERIALS

► **bathtub full of warm water**   ► **metal spoon**

PROCEDURE

1. Lie back in the tub so that your face is above water and your ears are underwater. **CAUTION: Get an adult's permission. Do not try this if you have ear problems.**
2. Lie quietly and listen. What do you hear?
3. With your ears still underwater, tap the spoon on the side of the tub. How would you describe the sound?
4. Sit up and tap the spoon in the same place. Now describe the sound.

CONCLUSIONS

How did the sounds you heard underwater compare with the sounds you heard above? Were you able to hear sounds underwater that you could not hear above? Why do you think things sound different underwater?

MAKING A MAP

How do they do it? The most important method of studying the ocean floor is called *echo sounding*. This is the same method that bats and porpoises use to navigate and to locate prey.

Scientists bounce a sound off the ocean floor. The sound is reflected back to a receiver. The time it takes for the echo to return indicates the depth of the water: the longer the time, the deeper the ocean at that point. A recorder puts each measurement on a graph that can then be used to produce a realistic map of the ocean floor. Another term for echo sounding is *sonar*, which is a combination of the words <u>so</u>und <u>n</u>avigation <u>and</u> <u>r</u>anging.

Sound travels almost four-and-a-half times faster in water than in air. Its average speed in water is about 1450 meters (4800 ft) per second. Differences in depth, water temperature, and salinity (amount of dissolved salt) can change this speed slightly. Scientists take even these slight differences into account to calculate their measurements as accurately as possible.

Fold

UNDERWATER VEHICLES

Bathyscaphes are a kind of submersible that can dive to the deepest parts of the ocean. They are made of extremely thick steel that can withstand great water pressure. In 1960 the bathyscaphe *Trieste* carried two men to a place almost 11,000 meters (36,000 ft) underwater. This place, the Mariana Trench, is located near the island of Guam and is the deepest known place in the Pacific Ocean. If Mt. Everest, the highest mountain on Earth, were placed in this trench, it would still be almost 2 kilometers (more than 1 mi) underwater!

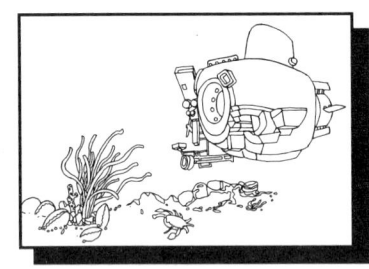

The submersible *ALVIN* helped oceanographers discover strange volcanic vents near the Galápagos Islands in 1977. Water from these vents reaches nearly 300°C (570°F)! Scientists aboard *ALVIN* also discovered tube worms and giant clams living around the vents.

Find Out

Use references to find out how the first oceanographers explored the sea. Describe to your class some of the early equipment that was used. Give a short demonstration of how ocean depth was measured before sonar.

Fold

MOUNTAINS AND VALLEYS UNDERWATER

Oceanographers have now mapped large areas of the oceans' floors. They have found that the continents and some islands are surrounded by an edge of land called a *continental shelf* that slopes down about 180 meters (600 ft) to the deep ocean floor.

Oceanographers have also discovered Earth's longest mountain range, the Mid-Ocean Ridge. This mountain ridge formed where two continental plates meet underwater.

The world's flattest plains are the *abyssal plains*. The plains surround the continent of Antarctica. These very flat, featureless plains lie below the Weddel Sea, which was named after the English navigator James Weddel, who explored Antarctica in the early 1800s.

Oceanographers have also found underwater volcanoes and huge mountains called *seamounts*. Deep canyons, called *submarine canyons*, have also been located. Finding all these features has given us a much better picture of the hidden ocean floor.

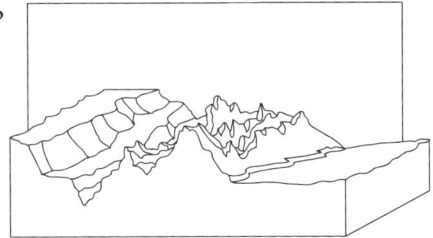

Science Fun

Black Holes

You may imagine that a black hole is a huge opening in space that pulls in everything around it. But a black hole is not really a hole at all. It is an extremely dense core left over from the explosion of a giant star, one with at least three times the mass of our sun. This core is made up of so much mass packed so tightly together that it produces the most powerful gravity in the universe. Black holes can capture light and even bend space itself!

LIFE AMONG THE STARS

Answers to Vocabulary Fun: 1. protostar, 2. supernova, 3. nebula, 4. star, 5. neutron, 6. red giant, 7. space probe, 8. white dwarf, 9. nuclear fusion, 10. black hole, 11. galaxy

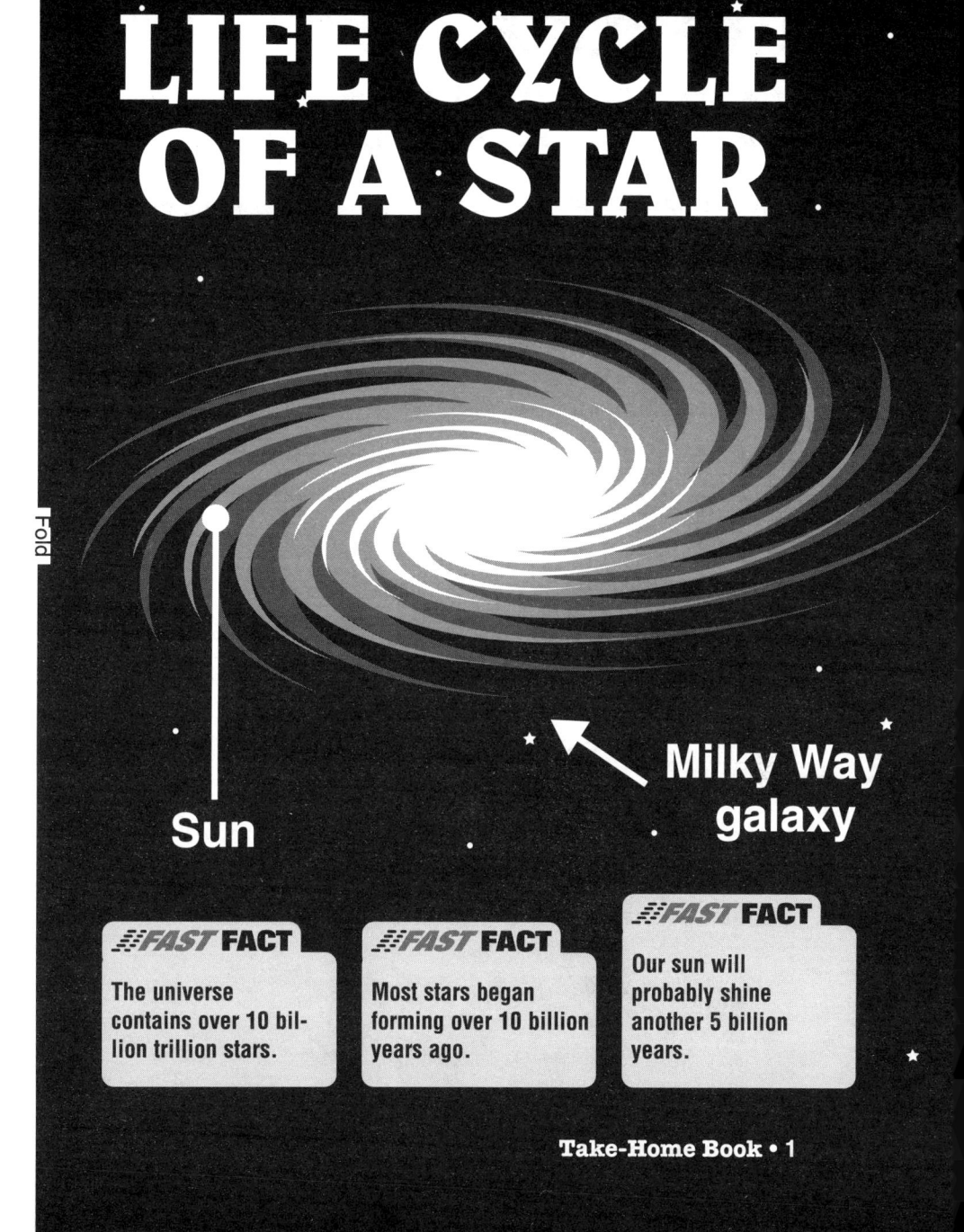

LIFE CYCLE OF A STAR

Sun

Milky Way galaxy

FAST FACT
The universe contains over 10 billion trillion stars.

FAST FACT
Most stars began forming over 10 billion years ago.

FAST FACT
Our sun will probably shine another 5 billion years.

LIFE CYCLE OF A STAR

Just as in the song we sang when we were little, we have all wondered about the stars. How big are they, and how far away? How were they formed? With the help of large new telescopes

and space probes, astronomers are beginning to answer some of our questions. By observing stars throughout the universe, they have discovered that, like people, stars have a life cycle. They are "born," they "grow," and they "die."

Stars are born in huge swirling clouds of dust and gas located in galaxies like our own Milky Way. A *galaxy* is a huge collection of stars held together by gravity. Within the galaxies these clouds, which are called *nebulae,* are almost invisible. Sometimes light from the stars nearby makes them glow. Sometimes astronomers can see them as dark patches passing in front of groups of stars. But nebulae are actually the "nurseries" of the stars.

"Twinkle, twinkle, little star. How I wonder what you are...."

VocabularyFun

Fill in the blanks in the following sentences.

1. A newborn star is a _____.

2. A _____ is an explosion of a dying star.

3. A _____ can be a nursery for stars.

4. A burning sphere of gases is a _____.

5. _____ stars are very dense.

6. When its fuel is used up, a star expands to become a _____ _____.

7. Cameras and instruments are sent on a _____ _____.

8. Our sun will probably become a _____ _____ at the end of its life.

9. Compressing atoms causes _____ _____.

10. Not even light can escape a _____ _____.

11. A huge collection of stars held together by gravity is a _____.

Answers on page 8

HOW A STAR HEATS UP

As a new star begins to form, it pulls large amounts of gases and dust into its core. These gases begin to get pressed together, causing the temperature of the newly formed star to rise. Do this activity to find out what happens when the gases in air are compressed.

MATERIALS

▶ **bicycle pump**

PROCEDURE

1. Ask a friend to cover one end of the pump with his or her hand. Now pump very hard for a few minutes.
2. Stop and put your hand on the outside of the tube. What do you feel?
3. Repeat the experiment. What do you feel this time?

CONCLUSIONS

What do you think is happening to the air inside the tube as you work the pump? What kind of change did the pumping cause? Why do you think the cores of newly formed stars grow so hot?

EXPLODING STARS

A sudden shock wave from a nearby star exploding or the pull of gravity from a star passing close to a nebula can begin the formation of a new star. Part of the cloud begins to swirl faster than before. It becomes very dense and its gravity starts to pull particles in from all around it. All this activity causes gases in the cloud to fall into a central core, called a *protostar*. Protostars are the newborns of the star world.

The size the new protostar takes depends on the mass available. It could remain small or grow to be a giant star. The largest star scientists know about is 1000 times the size of Earth's sun. The smallest star known is only about 20 kilometers (about 12 mi) in diameter.

The color of the new star depends on the temperature of its surface. Stars such as Rigel are a bright blue-white. Vega appears to be a brilliant white. Capella is yellow and Betelgeuse sends out glowing red rays. The red color of Betelgeuse is due to its low temperature, only 2800°C (5000°F). The hottest stars like blue Rigel burn at 28,000°C (50,000°F). The temperatures of the other stars fall somewhere between those of the red and blue stars.

Fold

NUCLEAR FUSION

When the gases fall into the core of a new star they are greatly compressed. This produces a huge amount of heat, making

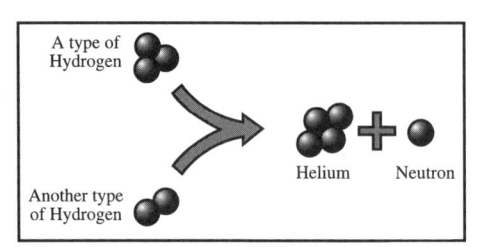

the newborn star start to glow. Eventually, the center of the new star heats up to over 1,100,000°C (2,000,000°F)! At this point the pressure inside the star is so enormous that atoms of hydrogen in the core begin to fuse—or stick together—and form helium. This *nuclear fusion* acts like a giant furnace inside the star. Now the star will burn steadily, just as our own sun does, for billions of years.

But all stars will use up the supply of hydrogen that fuels their furnaces. Medium- or small-sized stars like our sun can burn for billions of years. Larger stars, however, need more energy to keep burning. They are like large cars that need lots of fuel. They use up their supplies of hydrogen much faster than the smaller stars, so they have shorter lives—maybe only millions of years!

Make a mobile showing the stages in the life of a star like our sun. Show how the sizes of the smallest stars, such as white dwarfs, compare with the largest stars.

RED GIANTS

After a star's hydrogen is gone, its core becomes smaller and hotter. The heat fuses the helium atoms to form carbon atoms. The area around the core expands and the star becomes a *red giant*, one of the last stages in its life. In very large stars the hot core of the red giant gradually changes the carbon into heavier metals such as iron. Since these

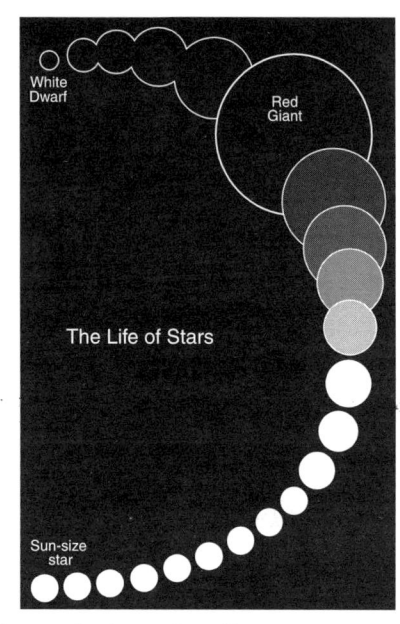

reactions do not produce energy, the red giant finally collapses and explodes. These star explosions are called *supernovae*.

Stars the size of our sun may change from a red giant to a *white dwarf*. As a white dwarf, a star like our sun would be compressed to the size of Earth. It would be so dense that 2 cubic centimeters ($\frac{1}{10}$ cu in.) might weigh 900 metric tons (1000 t)! Other stars, somewhat bigger than the sun, may change from red giants to *neutron stars*, which are even denser than white dwarfs. Or they may end up as *black holes*, whose enormous density causes a gravity so strong that nothing, not even light, can escape its pull!

Fold

ScienceFun

Insect Scuba Divers

Water beetles have to dive for their dinner. They eat other insects, tadpoles, and small fish that they find under water. Water beetles have flattened legs that work like paddles when they move through the water. They also have built-in air tanks to use when diving. Air is trapped between the beetles' hard outer wings and their soft bodies. When the water beetle dives for its food, it breathes stored air, just like a scuba diver!

MYSTERY WORD

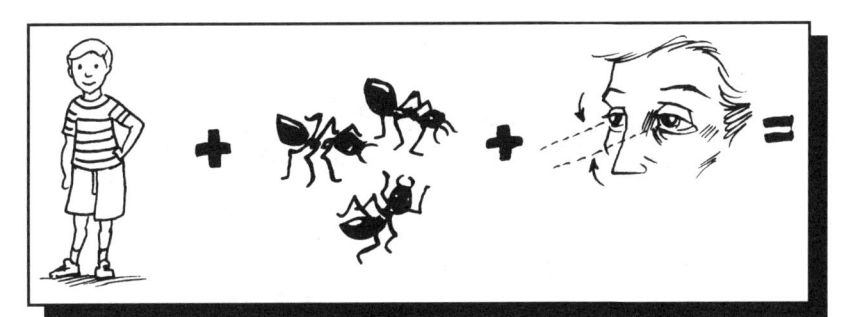

Answers to Vocabulary Fun: 1. Buoyant, 2. Scuba, 3. Life Jacket, 4. Buoyancy, 5. Density TITANIC

Answers to Science Fun: BUOYANCY

SINK OR SWIM

Life Jackets and How They Work

FAST FACT
Some life jackets are filled with *kapok*, "vegetable wool" from the fruit of a Malaysian tree.

FAST FACT
Modern scuba divers can explore at depths of 122 m (about 400 ft) under water.

FAST FACT
Ancient sea explorers used air-filled goatskin bladders and heavy stones to help them stay under water.

SINK OR SWIM

Have you ever laid your head back, stretched out your body, and floated on the surface of a swimming pool? If you have, you know that your body is naturally buoyant, or floatable. That's because the combination of muscles, fat, blood, and bones that make up your body is slightly less dense than water.

But in an emergency you may have trouble floating. If you are hurt, unconscious, or scared, you may have trouble swimming, even if you know how. Waves and cold water can make breathing difficult. You may get tired if you must wait for help. A life jacket can give you extra buoyancy to help keep your head above water. It could save your life.

Choosing a good life jacket or life vest is important. You should make sure it fits properly and that it is approved by the U.S. Coast Guard.

Vocabulary Fun

DIRECTIONS: Fill in the correct words. Then use the circled letters to solve the puzzle below.

1. To be floatable is to be _ _ _ _ _ ⃝⃝.

2. _ _ _ _ ⃝ divers carry their own air in tanks.

3. A _ ⃝ _ _ _ _ _ _ _ _ ⃝ helps you float in water.

4. A diver uses a _ _ _ _ _ _ ⃝ _ compensator to keep level.

5. To sink in water, you have to increase your
   _ _ _ _ _ ⃝ _ _.

List the circled letters in numerical order:

_ _ _ _ _ _ _ _

Now rearrange the letters to spell something that floated and then sank.

MAGIC EGG FLOAT

You have learned that when you mix two materials together the density of the mixture is between the densities of the two separate materials. Adding salt to water makes the new saltwater solution denser than plain water. How does this affect buoyancy? Try this activity to find out.

MATERIALS

▶ egg

▶ glass filled with 1 cup water

▶ 2 teaspoons salt

PROCEDURE

1. Place the egg in the glass of water. Does it float?
2. Now remove the egg and add 2 teaspoons of salt to the water. Stir.
3. Place the egg in the saltwater solution and observe. Does it float now?

CONCLUSIONS

How does the density of the egg compare with the density of plain water? How does it compare with salt water? Do you think your body would float more easily in the ocean or in a freshwater lake? Why?

HOW DO LIFE JACKETS WORK?

Life jackets or life vests are made of bright-colored canvas or nylon shells that can be seen easily in the water. They are filled with materials that are low in density, such as plastic foam, fiberglass, plant fibers, or cork. Some have compartments that can be inflated with air. When you wear a jacket made from these materials, the water beneath you is more dense than you are. It pushes you up toward the less-dense air. This buoyant force is stronger than the force of gravity!

Life Jacket Types

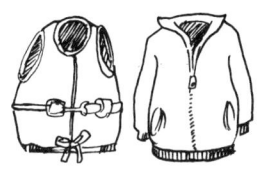

Type 1: Best for open, rough water when rescue may be slow. Turns unconscious wearers face up.

Type 2: Good for calmer water, where rescue may be quick. Less bulky than Type 1.

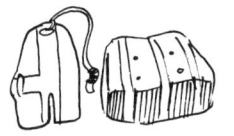

Type 3: More comfortable than other types. Best for calm water where rescue is close by.

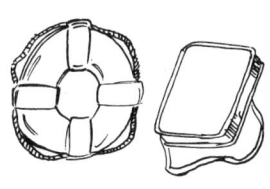

Type 4: Throwable life preserver. Must be used near boat.

Fold

HOW DIVERS MOVE UNDER WATER

Divers who use snorkels must stay on the surface of the water. Because snorkels—breathing tubes with mouthpieces—must extend up into the air, these divers welcome the buoyant force of water. It keeps them swimming on top of the water while they look through their face masks to watch the underwater world below.

Buoys are hollow metal or plastic floats that are used as markers in the water. Use a dictionary or an encyclopedia to find out about the kinds of buoys. What different purposes do they have? Design your own buoy from a juice can or a plastic soft drink bottle. What will keep your buoy from floating away?

SCUBA DIVERS

Scuba divers must work against their buoyancy to travel downward in the water. To increase their bodies' density, they wear belts with weights of lead or sand. These make their bodies as dense as water, so that they can move up and down more easily. Rubber flippers help them swim, and foam rubber suits protect them against cold water. They carry their own air supply in a tank.

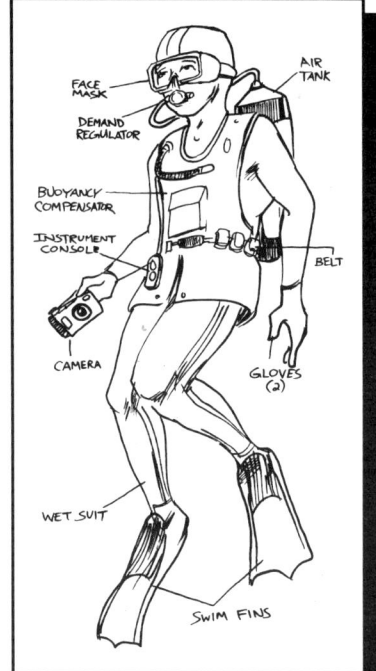

When divers reach the depth they want, they use a piece of equipment called a *buoyancy compensator*. This equipment looks like an inflatable jacket with an air tank attached to the back. Inflating the jacket with air causes the diver to stop moving downward. If a diver adds more air to the compensator, he or she will begin to rise again. Divers usually try to control their buoyancy so they can stay at one level for a while.

Find Out

What is the meaning of the term *scuba*? Use reference books or an encyclopedia to find out. Who invented the first scuba diving equipment?

Science Fun

The "Thermometer" Bird

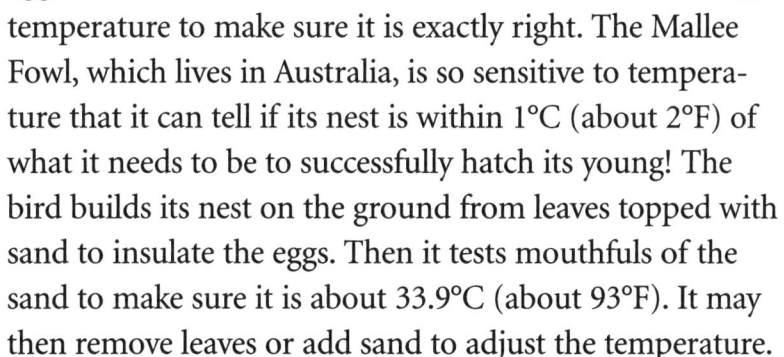

Imagine a bird that not only builds a unique nest to incubate its eggs, but also takes the nest's temperature to make sure it is exactly right. The Mallee Fowl, which lives in Australia, is so sensitive to temperature that it can tell if its nest is within 1°C (about 2°F) of what it needs to be to successfully hatch its young! The bird builds its nest on the ground from leaves topped with sand to insulate the eggs. Then it tests mouthfuls of the sand to make sure it is about 33.9°C (about 93°F). It may then remove leaves or add sand to adjust the temperature.

HELP THE HEAT WAVE!

This little heat wave needs to get to the ice cube in order to melt it. Can you find a way for it to travel through this maze?

Answers to Vocabulary Fun: 2. insulation, 3. conduction, 4. thermos, 5. blubber, 6. insulate, 7. vacuum, 8. heat

INSULATION

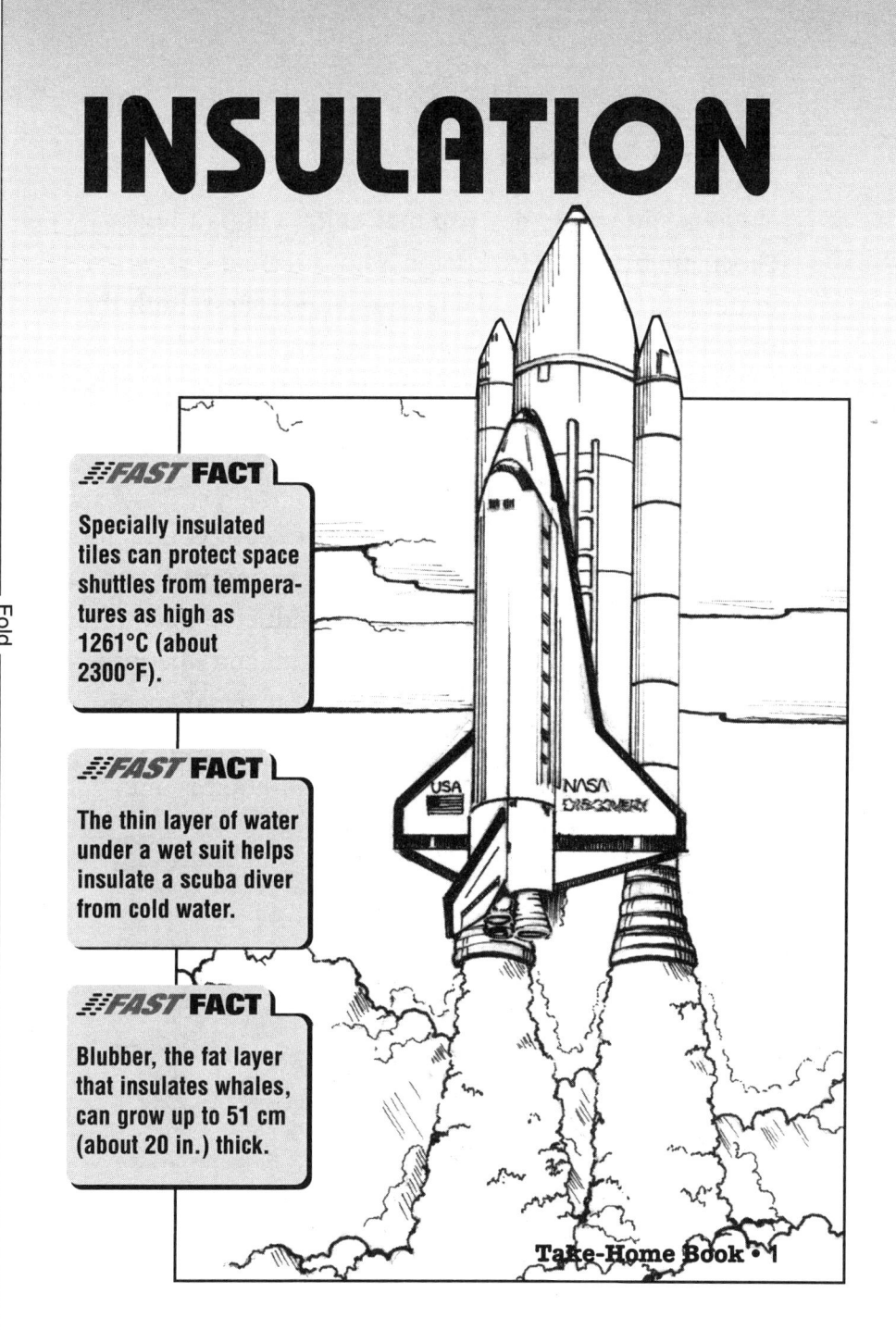

FAST FACT

Specially insulated tiles can protect space shuttles from temperatures as high as 1261°C (about 2300°F).

FAST FACT

The thin layer of water under a wet suit helps insulate a scuba diver from cold water.

FAST FACT

Blubber, the fat layer that insulates whales, can grow up to 51 cm (about 20 in.) thick.

Fold

INSULATION

On a cold winter day you may enjoy a cup of hot chocolate from a thermos. On a hot summer day, you're grateful for a cold soft drink from an ice chest. Both the thermos and the ice chest are doing the same job—insulating your drinks from changes in temperature. To *insulate* means to prevent thermal energy from passing into or out of something.

Materials that are good insulators are poor conductors of thermal energy. Often they contain many small pockets of air, which is also a very poor conductor. Examples of good insulators are cork, plastic foam, and fiberglass. Other materials prevent the transfer of thermal energy by radiation. They do this by reflecting the thermal energy back toward its source. Aluminum foil is one material that does this.

VocabularyFun

Put the words into the puzzle. The first word has been done for you.

4 letters	6 letters	7 letters
heat	vacuum	blubber
		thermos

8 letters	9 letters	10 letters
insulate	radiation	insulation
		conduction

Answers on page 8

WHY IS WOOL SO WARM?

Many cold-weather clothes are made of wool. Find out why with these activities.

MATERIALS

▶ **wool mitten**

▶ **drinking glass**

▶ **refrigerator**

▶ **thermometer**

▶ **scrap of wool and scrap of cotton**

PROCEDURE

1. Place the mitten and the drinking glass in the refrigerator for at least fifteen minutes. Take them out and see if one is colder than the other. Use a thermometer and hold it against each object. Record the temperatures.
2. Now take the scrap of wool and use a pencil to push it gently to the bottom of a glass of water. Then let it rise to the top of the water and gently push it down again. What do you see? Repeat with the cotton cloth scrap.

CONCLUSIONS

Which felt colder—the glass or the mitten? Which object is a better insulator? What did you see when you pushed the wool down? What does this tell you about wool? About cotton? How does it show you which is a better insulating material?

THE FIRST THERMOS

The first thermos—called a vacuum bottle—was invented in 1892 by a scientist named Sir James Dewar. He had changed some gases into liquids and needed a container that would keep them very cold. His design included two glass bottles—a smaller one fitting inside a larger one. Dewar removed air from the small space between the two bottles, which created a *vacuum* (VAK•yoom). Vacuums are empty spaces that contain nothing, not even air. They are even better insulators than air because they contain no molecules to transfer thermal energy.

But Dewar knew that thermal energy could still pass through the vacuum by radiation. So he covered the outside of the inner bottle with a silvery material. This material acted like a mirror and reflected the thermal energy back to its source. Then he melted the glass bottles together at their tops and added a thick cork stopper. An outer metal case completed his invention.

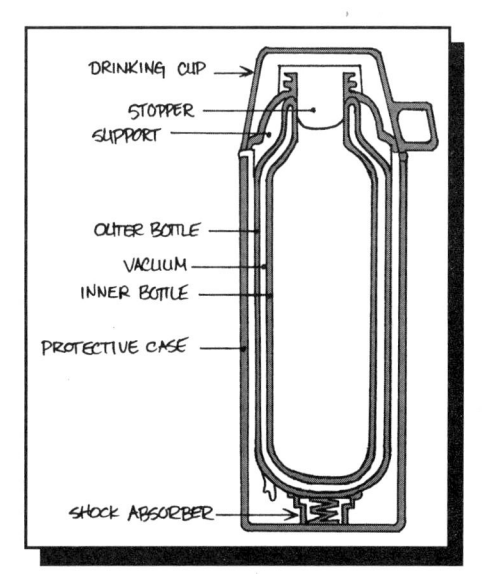

ICE CHESTS

Most ice chests are made of plastic or plastic foam. Plastic ice chests may have double walls filled with plastic foam. This foam contains small bubbles of air, which help prevent conduction of thermal energy. It stops thermal energy from leaking into the cooler, melting the ice, and warming the drinks and food inside. What happens if you open the ice chest frequently? On a hot day at the beach or camping you may want to put your ice chest in the shade. What kind of thermal energy transfer does this prevent?

Find Out

Asbestos is a material that once was commonly used for insulation. Use an encyclopedia or a computer to find out how asbestos is formed and where it is found. Why is it no longer used in homes and other buildings?

Fold

INSULATION KEEPS US COMFORTABLE

Homes of all kinds need insulation to help prevent the transfer of thermal energy. Igloos made of ice blocks can stop thermal energy from passing outside. Straw-thatched huts in tropical lands can keep people cool by blocking thermal energy radiating from the sun. Other homes may use foam or fiberglass to line roof shingles or fill the insides of walls. Windows with double glass panes have an air space that helps stop thermal energy from leaking outside.

Our bodies also need insulation for comfort in cold weather. Coats stuffed with goose down or artificial fibers keep us warm in winter. Wool sweaters and mittens protect against cold weather. Layers of light clothing that form air pockets slow the loss of thermal energy better than a single heavy garment.

Think & Do

Build a simple model of a shelter used by people in a tropical country and one used by people in a colder country. Find out what sorts of materials might be used in their construction. Explain to your class how different types of insulation work for each house.

Science **Fun**

Fiddle and Drum

Did you know that some insects are musicians? The katydid scrapes its right wing against notches on its left wing just like a fiddler slides the bow across violin strings. And, as a fiddler may play a tune for his sweetheart, the katydid calls its mate with the "music" it makes.

Cicadas (sih•KAY•duhz) also court their mates with the buzzing sounds they make on their very own drums! Male cicadas have a drum-like area on their abdomens. Muscles attached to the "drum-skin" pull it in, then let it snap back. This quick snapping may vibrate the skin 480 times a second, causing a shrill buzzing sound

A RIDDLE IN RHYME

I'm important in sports,
I'm important in song.
Sometimes I'm wide,
Sometimes I'm wrong.

I may start a concert
Or win a close game.
I'm high or I'm low,
Do you know my name?

Answer to Science Fun: Pitch

Answers to Vocabulary Fun: 1. sound, 2. echo, 3. vibrates, 4. echolocation, 5. Ultrasonic, 6. infrasonic

HOW ANIMALS USE SOUND

FAST FACT
Some spiders can hear things that vibrate as slowly as 20 times per second and as fast as 45,000 times per second.

FAST FACT
Some fish can both produce and hear sounds with their swim bladders.

FAST FACT
Dolphins have no outer ears but can hear sounds eight times higher than humans can.

HOW ANIMALS
USE SOUND

More than 200 years ago an Italian scientist named Lazzaro Spallanzani performed an experiment. Spallanzani wanted to know how bats navigated in the dark. He believed that bats could not see well but somehow used another sense to move around in the dark without bumping into things.

To test his idea, he strung a maze of silk threads in a dark room. When he released some bats that had been blinded, they flew easily through the maze, never tangling in the threads! Then Spallanzani plugged the ears of some other bats with wax. When he put these bats in the room, they became hopelessly snarled in the threads! What do you think Spallanzani concluded?

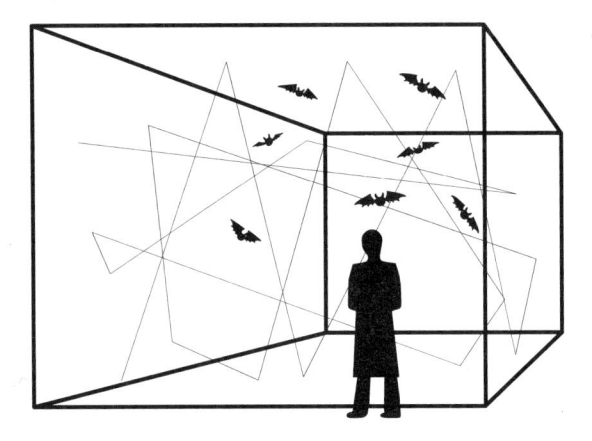

Vocabulary Fun

Unscramble these words:

BRAVTIES _____

TLRUANOCSI _____

RSOFNINACI _____

CATLOCHOENIO _____

NDUSO _____

COEH _____

Now use these words to fill in the blanks below.

1. _____ is a series of vibrations you can hear.

2. An _____ is a reflection of sound.

3. Something that moves back and forth _____.

4. Using echos to find something is called _____.

5. _____ means vibrations that are too fast and high pitched for humans to hear.

6. The rumblings of an elephant are _____ sounds.

Answers on page 8

CAN YOU HEAR A PIN DROP?

We know that elephants can hear infrasonic sounds from miles away. Do this activity to test how well human ears can hear a very small sound from a distance.

MATERIALS

▶ **straight pin**
▶ **drinking glass**
▶ **paper and pencil**
▶ **measuring tape or yardstick**

PROCEDURE

1. Sit at a table or desk with the pin and the glass in front of you. Have a partner stand nearby with his or her back to you.
2. Hold the pin near the top of the glass and drop it onto the table. Ask your partner to move two steps farther away, and drop the pin again.
3. Repeat the procedure as long as your partner reports hearing the sound. Always drop the pin from the same height.
4. Report how far your partner must move before he or she can no longer hear the pin drop.

CONCLUSIONS

How far away was your partner when he or she could no longer hear the pin drop? Animals who are hunters have very keen hearing. What animals might be able to hear the pin drop better than you or your partner?

ULTRASONIC SOUND

Today we know that to find their way the bats were using an ability called *echolocation*. Echolocation is the use of echoes to find the location of an object. Bats listen to echoes of their own high-pitched cries in order to navigate or to find prey in the dark. Most of their cries cannot be heard by humans. We hear sounds caused by vibrations of between 20 and 20,000 times per second. But bats' cries are *ultrasonic* (uhl•truh•SAHN•ik), which means they are caused by vibrations faster than 20,000 times per second. In fact, their squeaks and cries are caused by vibrations as fast as 120,000 times per second!

Ultrasonic sound works well for bats because it reflects in a fairly straight path, like a flashlight beam. The bat's brain can pick out the patterns of the echoes and form a "sound picture." This "picture" can tell the bat the distance and direction to a nearby cave wall or to the delicious moth it is chasing for dinner.

INFRASONIC SOUND

You may have heard an elephant at a zoo or circus make a loud trumpeting sound with its trunk. Elephants can also snort, bark, or growl to show fear or anger or to greet another group of elephants. But the most amazing sounds made by elephants are very low rumblings that people cannot even hear! The rumblings are *infrasonic* sounds caused by vibrations of from 14 to 35 times per second. These vibrations are as slow as earthquake rumbles far below the ground!

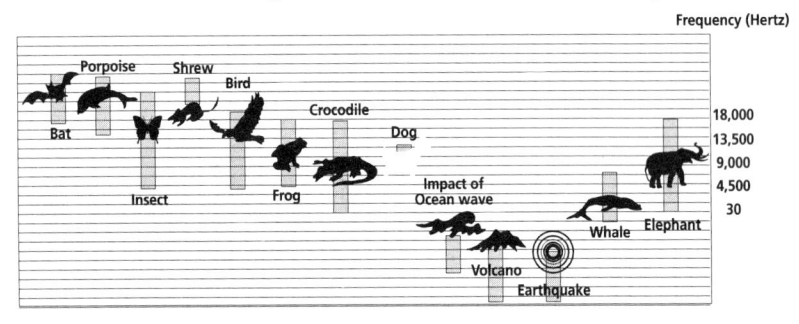

Think & Do

Make a bar graph showing the ranges of sound heard by different animals, including bats, elephants, dolphins, cats, dogs, insects, whales, and any others for which you can find this information. On your chart, show how the human range of hearing compares with the hearing ranges of these animals.

ELEPHANT COMMUNICATION

Scientists studying elephants in Africa found out about the infrasonic sounds by observing how the animals behaved in herds. They noticed that a whole group of elephants would suddenly stop still and seem to listen intently. They also noticed slight vibrations and fluttering in the air.

When they saw that family groups of elephants seemed to travel in parallel paths for days, they realized that herds might be communicating with sounds that humans can't hear.

Find Out

Howler monkeys make very unpleasant noises. Use an encyclopedia or reference book to find out where howler monkeys live and how they got their name. From how far away can the howler monkey be heard?

Science Fun

DRIVERLESS CARS?

Not only may cars of the future have different kinds of engines, they may also be able to run without a driver! Cars may be completely run by computers on computerized highway systems. We may program our cars for certain destinations, then sit back and relax while the car drives us there. Computer sensors would keep the car from touching other vehicles, let alone having an accident. And we might be able to travel safely at speeds as high as 320 kilometers (about 200 mi) per hour!

RIDDLES

▶ **Q:** Why does the electric car love to go shopping?

A: *Because it knows it can charge everything.*

▶ **Q:** Why did the electric car run away from home?

A: *Because it wanted to join the circuit.*

THE TROUBLE WITH
SOLAR POWERED CARS....

I HATE CLOUDY DAYS!

Answer to Vocabulary Fun: Electric cars are the future.

ELECTRICITY AND MAGNETISM IN TRANSPORTATION

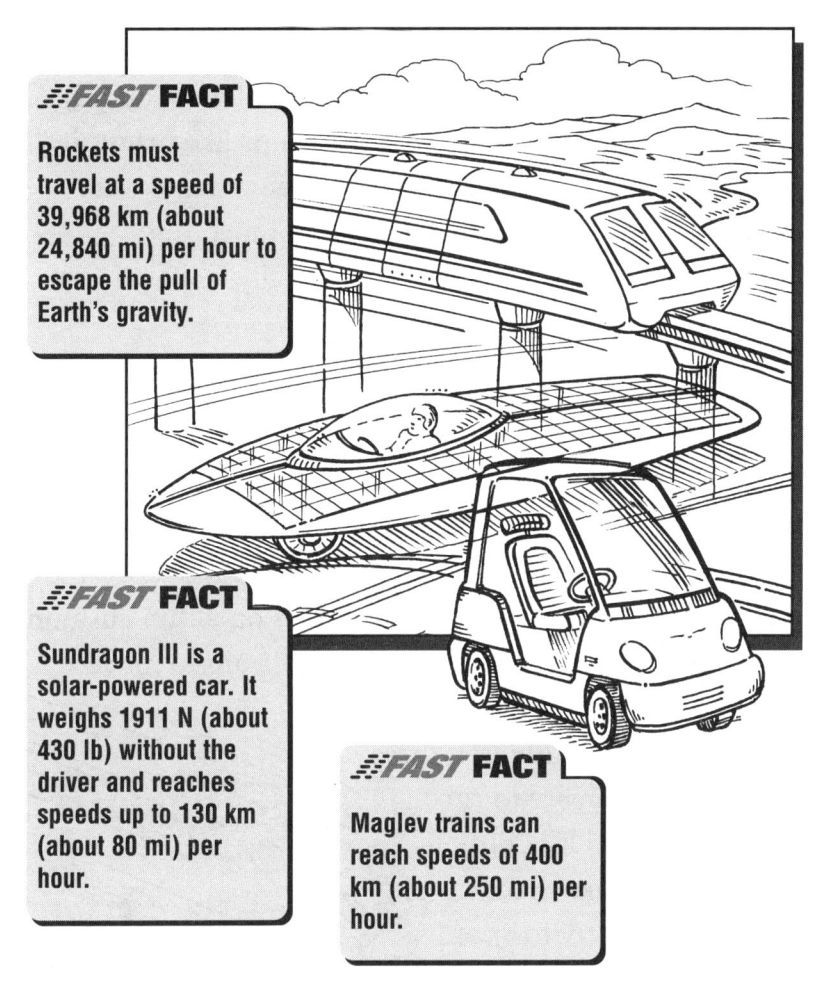

FAST FACT
Rockets must travel at a speed of 39,968 km (about 24,840 mi) per hour to escape the pull of Earth's gravity.

FAST FACT
Sundragon III is a solar-powered car. It weighs 1911 N (about 430 lb) without the driver and reaches speeds up to 130 km (about 80 mi) per hour.

FAST FACT
Maglev trains can reach speeds of 400 km (about 250 mi) per hour.

Fold

ELECTROMAGNETIC
TRANSPORTATION

How would you like to ride on a train that travels at speeds of 160 to 320 kilometers (about 100 to 200 mi) per hour and floats on air? If this sounds like magic, it's not! Some of these trains—called maglev trains—are actually running in Japan, Germany, France, and England. *Maglev* stands for "magnetically levitated." *Levitated* means "floating on air."

The bottoms of maglev trains and the tops of the tracks they run on are lined with strong electromagnets. The north poles of the electromagnets on the train face the north poles of the electromagnets on the tracks, so they push away from each other. They push so hard they push the train up off the track. It rides on a thin cushion of air. Riding on air allows the maglev train to move much faster and more smoothly than ordinary trains. Although these trains are expensive to run, their speed and lack of pollution may make them a very popular way to travel in the future.

Vocabulary Fun

Read the words in the word bank. Find and circle each word hidden in the puzzle.

levitation	maglev
plasma	ions
electric	hybrids

```
H  L  B  I  R  O  Z  A  B  O  G
C  I  E  B  Y  D  O  R  E  F  V
J  T  J  V  S  Q  U  E  L  H  X
H  Y  B  R  I  D  S  E  E  H  A
P  E  C  K  O  T  M  A  C  Y  Z
T  U  F  D  N  D  A  Z  T  U  G
G  E  K  C  S  L  G  T  R  N  Q
D  I  A  M  S  A  L  P  I  F  Y
K  B  M  V  O  R  E  M  C  O  W
A  L  A  K  W  S  V  I  N  R  N
```

Bright Idea

Circle the first letter (*e*) below. Skip two letters and circle again. Continue to skip two and circle. Then write the letters in order to make a sentence.

e a r l b c e g q c m z t d o r v w i z q c e n c f i a b d r s
n s z w a c e r o n e r q t h p h i o e w r f i t u e t t o m u
c o r y i e

Answers on page 8

MAGNETS AND CARS: SEE HOW THEY RUN

As you have learned, powerful electromagnets can lift maglev trains above their tracks. Do this activity to see how magnets could affect cars.

MATERIALS

▶ **2 small bar magnets** ▶ **2 small toy cars**
▶ **masking or other strong tape**

PROCEDURE

1. Tape bar magnets to tops of cars. Tape the magnets so that their north poles are at the fronts of the cars.
2. Roll the cars toward each other. Try to make the front ends of the cars meet. What happens?
3. Now try to roll the cars closely past each other as if they were passing on a highway. What happens to the paths of the cars?
4. Now place one car behind the other so that the front bumper of one is near the back bumper of the other. What happens?

CONCLUSIONS

How did the magnets affect the movements of the cars in Steps 2, 3, and 4? Can you think of ways the magnets might be used to solve traffic problems? What problems might the use of magnets on cars cause?

PLASMA POWER

Electrically powered rockets may also become popular in the future. Most rockets now use solid or liquid fuel to move. But another way to power rockets is to heat a gas in the engine to temperatures above 50,000°C (about 90,000°F). This turns the gas into a state of matter called *plasma*. Plasma contains charged particles called *ions*, which are atoms that have lost or gained electrons.

When the ions are passed through electrical conductors, they can produce enough power to slowly speed up a rocket. This kind of power cannot propel a heavy rocket into space, but it can run a rocket engine in space for much longer periods of time.

Fluorescent lights also contain plasma, which gives off light when electrons and ions bump together.

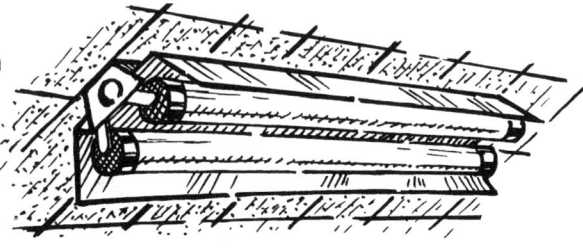

ELECTRIC CARS IN THE FUTURE?

Electric cars are an old idea that may become very important in the future. Some of the first cars made were powered by electricity. In fact, in the late 1800s, more Americans drove "electrics" than gasoline-fueled cars. But there were problems with electric cars. They could only travel 30 to 65 kilometers (about 20 to 40 mi) before needing to have their batteries recharged. They were more expensive to run than gasoline-powered autos, and they generally traveled at speeds of only 19 kilometers (about 12 mi) per hour. By the 1920s gasoline-fueled cars had replaced electric cars because they were cheaper, faster, and more convenient.

But some people believe that using electricity to run cars could solve many problems we have today. Electric cars don't use up scarce petroleum resources. They don't release exhaust fumes that pollute our atmosphere. And they provide a much quieter ride than gasoline-fueled autos.

Think & Do

Make a list of electric-powered vehicles that we use today. HINT: Think of vehicles that are used in sports and recreation, city transportation, and for specialized services.

HYBRIDS

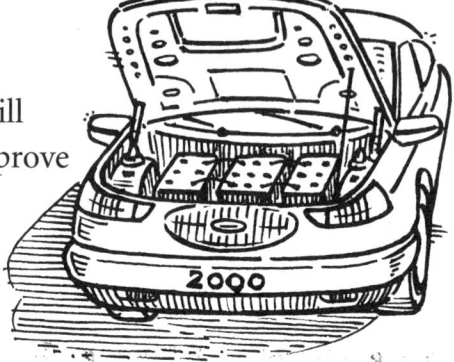

Carmakers today are still trying to develop and improve electric cars, which may someday work well enough to replace gasoline-powered vehicles. Some of the newer models can travel up to 110 kilometers (about 70 mi) between battery recharges.

One answer to the problems of both electric and gasoline-powered cars may be to build cars that combine the best qualities of each. Models of such cars, called *hybrids*, were first tried in the 1970s. Hybrid cars have an electric engine and batteries, along with a gasoline engine that can also be used to recharge the batteries. Right now the new hybrids are very expensive. But manufacturers hope to learn how to build them more cheaply, so more people will be able to afford them.

Find Out

Some engineers have been experimenting with solar-powered cars. Use an encyclopedia or other reference books to find out how fast these cars can go and how far they can travel. Explain briefly how these cars use energy from the sun to run.

Fold

Harcourt

Science Fun

Rocket-Powered Planes

In 1957, the *X-1* became the first rocket airplane to make a *supersonic* (faster than sound) flight. Later, in 1967, the *X-15* flew more than 6 times the speed of sound. Now scientists are working on new *space-planes*, which, unlike most rockets, would be reusable. In the atmosphere these planes could take in air to burn fuel like normal planes. In space they would burn liquid hydrogen and oxygen as rockets do.

SOLVE THIS CODE

Use the code key below to find the name of a scientist who developed the liquid-fueled rocket. Place the letters for the numbers in the blanks.

Example: 24 would be C.

9 - 12 - 25 - 22 - 9 - 7   _ _ _ _ _ _

19.   _ .

20 - 12 - 23 - 23 - 26 - 9 - 23   _ _ _ _ _ _ _

A-26	E-22	I-18	M-14	Q-10	U-6	Y-2
B-25	F-21	J-17	N-13	R-9	V-5	Z-1
C-24	G-20	K-16	O-12	S-8	W-4	
D-23	H-19	L-15	P-11	T-7	X-3	

Answer to Science Fun: Robert H. Goddard

Answers to Vocabulary Fun: 1. F inertia, 2. E oxidizer, 3. D gravity, 4. B accelerate, 5. C thrust, 6. A propellant.

Unit F • Chapter 1 TH69

8 • **Take-Home Book**

HOW ROCKETS WORK

Fold

FAST FACT

The Saturn V rocket, one of the most powerful launch vehicles ever built, weighed 26,656,000 N (about 6,000,000 lb).

FAST FACT

In 1961, a rocket carried the first human, the Russian cosmonaut Yuri A. Gagarin, into orbit around Earth.

FAST FACT

Chinese armies fired rockets in battle in 1232 A.D. They may have been the first to use rockets.

Take-Home Book • 1

HOW ROCKETS WORK

Rockets can power spaceships far into space or shoot fireworks into the night sky. Fuel burning inside a rocket chamber forms hot gases that push out in all directions inside the rocket. The only place the expanding gases can escape is out the bottom (nozzle) end of the rocket. The powerful release of these gases causes an upward force on the rocket called *thrust*.

Thrust is based on a law of motion described by the scientist Sir Isaac Newton, who lived over 300 years ago. Newton showed that when an action force is applied, a *reaction force*, or equal force in the opposite direction, also takes place. This is the third law of motion. In the case of a rocket, the action force is the release of hot gases. The reaction force is the upward thrust on the rocket.

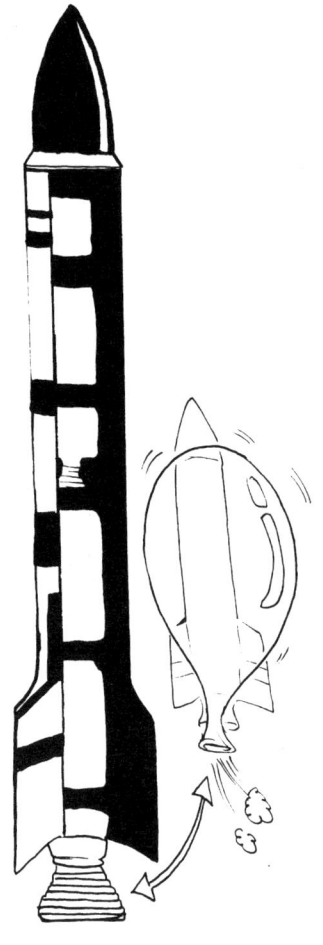

Vocabulary Fun

Unscramble the following words and then match them to the definitions below.

A. E L R T P A N O P L _ _ _ _ _ _ _ _ _ _

B. L E E C A C A R T E _ _ _ _ _ _ _ _ _ _

C. S T U T R H _ _ _ _ _ _ _ _

D. T R I G A Y V _ _ _ _ _ _ _ _

E. D E X Z O I R I _ _ _ _ _ _ _ _

F. T R A I N I E _ _ _ _ _ _ _ _

1. An object's resistance to changes in movement

_____

2. A chemical that supplies oxygen

_____

3. The pull of Earth on an object

_____

4. To change the speed of an object in motion

_____

5. The upward push on a rocket

_____

6. The combination of a fuel and an oxidizer

_____

Answer on page 8

Fold

BE AN "EGGSPERT"

You have learned that inertia is the resistance of an object to changes in movement. Do this activity to show how inertia can help you tell the difference between a raw egg and a hard-boiled egg.

MATERIALS

▶ one raw egg   ▶ two small plates

▶ one hard-boiled egg

PROCEDURE

1. Place each egg on a plate.
2. Touch each egg with your finger to start it spinning. Note which egg is easier to spin.
3. Now touch each egg with your finger to stop the spinning. Note which egg is easier to stop.

CONCLUSIONS

Remember that the yolk in a raw egg floats in the liquid white. In the hard-boiled egg, the yolk is held in one place by the solid white. Which egg was easier to spin? Why? Which egg was harder to stop spinning? Why? How does this demonstrate the law of inertia?

THE LAWS OF MOTION

Two other laws of motion can help us understand how rockets work. The first law of motion states that an object at rest will not move unless an outside force acts on it. Without the rush of hot gases from inside it, the rocket would remain on the ground. The law also says that once an object is moving, it will continue to move in one direction unless an outside force changes its movement. This first law describes *inertia* (in•ER•shuh), which is the resistance of an object to changes in movement.

A ball pitched toward home plate cannot travel toward first base unless the force of the bat changes its direction.

According to the second law of motion, the greater the amount of force on an object, the more it will *accelerate*. To accelerate means to change speed or change direction. A rocket will continue to speed up as long as its engine has fuel to burn. The stronger the engine, or the greater the force of the burning gases, the faster the rocket will travel.

Fold

ROCKET POWER

Rockets need lots of power to travel out into space and away from the pull of Earth's gravity. They must travel 40,000 kilometers (about 24,856 mi) per hour to escape this pull. This speed is called the *escape velocity.*

In order to travel fast enough, rocket engines burn special fuels. One kind is solid fuel, which can be stored easily for long periods of time. These fuels are chemicals that form a thick, rubbery substance inside the rocket. Liquid fuels, the other type, can provide more thrust, but are harder to store because they require very low temperatures to keep from changing back into gases. Most rockets that carry astronauts or satellites into space use liquid fuels.

Build a model rocket that uses a balloon for power. Construct it so that air escaping from the balloon provides the thrust to propel the rocket into the air. CAUTION: Launch your rocket in a safe place outdoors. Never shoot the rocket toward another person.

BLAST OFF!

Rocket fuels need oxygen to burn. Since there is no oxygen in space, the rocket carries a chemical called an *oxidizer* (AHKS•ih•dyz•er) along to provide the necessary oxygen. The combination of the oxidizer and the fuel is called the *propellant* (proh•PEL•uhnt). Rockets require more propellant when traveling through Earth's atmosphere than they do when flying through space. Gases in the atmosphere cause friction, which slows the rocket. Once the rocket is out in space, less propellant is needed and the rocket continues to speed up until its fuel is used up.

Space rockets must carry enough fuel for high speeds and long flights. To do this, the rocket is divided into sections called *stages.* Each stage has its own fuel tank and rocket engines and is discarded after the stage's fuel is used. This lightens the load of the final stage and allows it to travel farther.

Find Out

Use reference materials to find out how rockets are used to study Earth's atmosphere and weather. How do the rockets send information back to scientists? Share what you learn with your class.

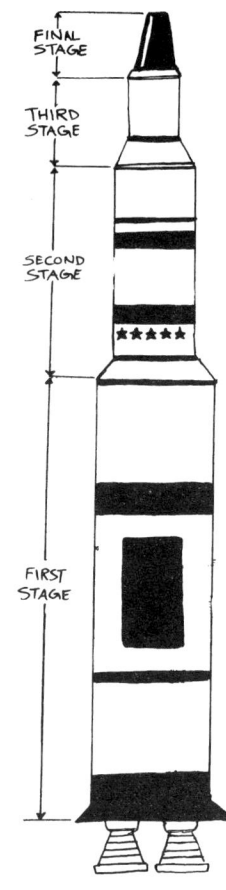

FINAL STAGE

THIRD STAGE

SECOND STAGE

FIRST STAGE

Science Fun

A WEIRD MACHINE

One of the strangest examples of the use of gears was found in the wreck of an ancient Greek ship. This machine, which was a kind of mechanical calendar, contained 25 bronze gearwheels arranged in a group or "train." The gears controlled pointers that showed future positions of the sun, moon, and stars. The calendar was probably built about 100 A.D.

MECHANICAL STRENGTH

Show your strength, actually mechanical strength, by asking a friend to grab the handle of a floor broom. Ask him or her to not allow the broom to turn. When you turn the head of the broom it will be impossible for your friend to resist the turning. The head of the broom becomes a crank that will turn the handle. That's mechanical strength working for you!

Answers to Vocabulary Fun: Across 1. Shaft, 4. Worm, 5. Gear, 7. Axle, 9. Helical, 10. Work Down 1. Spur, 2. Torque, 3. Bevel, 6. Gear ratio, 8. Pinion

HOW GEARS WORK

FAST FACT
Some of the tiniest gears made move the bristles of electric toothbrushes.

FAST FACT
The derailleur gear system for bicycles was invented in 1911.

FAST FACT
One of the earliest uses of gears was in a water clock built in Egypt in the first century A.D.

HOW GEARS WORK

When you bicycle to school, open a can of soup, or ride a roller coaster, you are using machines that have gears. Gears are wheels with teeth along the edges. The teeth push against the teeth of other wheels as they turn. They transfer motion and power from one part of a machine to another to help us do work.

If you look at a manual can opener, you can see an example of a simple gear. Hold the opener in one hand and turn the handle with the other. **Be careful of the blade!** Do you see the gears move? They help transfer the motion and force of your hand turning the handle to the movement of the blade along the edge of the can.

A gear is really a combination of two simple machines: a wheel and axle and a lever. The axle of the gearwheel is called the *shaft*. Often, the shaft is connected to a power source such as an electric motor. When one gear pushes against another, its force and motion cause the second gear to turn in the opposite direction.

Vocabulary Fun

GEARS

CLUES

ACROSS

1. the axle of the gear
4. type of gear that looks like a screw
5. a wheel with teeth
7. rod attached to a wheel
9. type of gear with twisted teeth
10. results when a force produces movement

DOWN

1. simplest type of gear
2. turning force
3. type of gear found in an egg beater
6. relationship of the sizes of gears in a pair
8. smaller gear in a pair

Answers on page 8

FINDING A GEAR RATIO

MATERIALS

- ▶ bicycle, any type
- ▶ masking tape or chalk

PROCEDURE

1. Turn the bike upside down. Place a piece of tape or a chalk mark anywhere on the rear tire of the bike.
2. Move the pedals one full turn. Note how many times the wheel rotates. Use the mark to help you count.
3. Knowing the number of rotations of the wheel per turn of the pedals allows you to calculate the gear ratio of the bike. If the wheel turns five times for every one pedal turn, the gear ratio is 5 to 1, or 5:1.
4. If the bike has more than one gear size, try this procedure using a smaller gear, and then a larger gear. Record your results. If the bike has only one speed, try this activity with another bike and compare it with the first one.

CONCLUSIONS

How did the gear ratios of the high and low speeds compare? If you used two different bikes, how did the gear ratios of the two compare? What would it mean if someone told you the gear ratio of his or her bike was 1:3?

WORKING TOGETHER

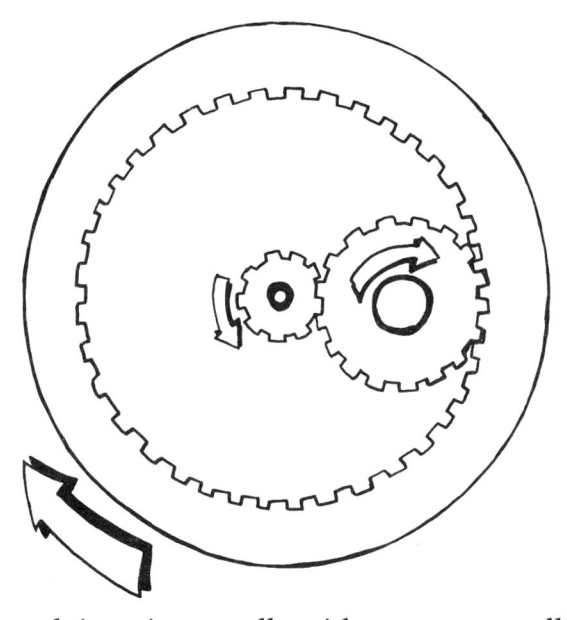

Gears work in pairs, usually with one gear smaller than the other. The smaller gear, which is called the *pinion* (PIN•yuhn), turns faster than the larger one. The difference in the sizes of the gears and the number of teeth on each determines their power and speed. For instance, if the larger gear has 50 teeth and the pinion has 10, we say they have a *gear ratio* of 5:1. This means that for every turn the larger gear makes, the pinion will rotate five times. It also means that the larger gear moves with five times the force of the smaller gear. This turning force is called the *torque* (TAWRK).

Fold

GEARS AT WORK

Gears can either speed up or slow down the operation of a machine. When you ride a multi-speed bicycle, you can change gears to control the speed and the amount of force you need to pedal the bike. If you are on level ground, you don't need much force, so you ride in a higher gear. This means your bike wheels travel faster with fewer turns of the pedals. When you are going uphill, you switch to a lower gear. Then your pedaling makes more force, but the speed of the wheels is less. You pedal faster, but the wheel has increased torque to go up the hill.

Write a diary entry for one day that names every machine you use that has gears. Don't forget kitchen equipment, toys, and transportation. Some gears are hidden inside machines. If you aren't sure if a machine has gears, check the manual that comes with it, or ask an adult.

DIFFERENT KINDS OF GEARS

People have developed many kinds of gears to do different kinds of work. The simplest type of gear is the *spur gear*, which you saw in the can opener. Spur gears have straight teeth and parallel shafts. They are also used in mechanical clocks and watches. *Helical* (HEL•ih•kuhl) *gears* have twisted teeth. They are quieter than spur gears and are used in high-speed machines such as helicopters and jet engines. *Bevel gears* have straight teeth set at an angle to the axle. Egg beaters and power drills contain bevel gears. *Worm gears* look a little like screws. They can reduce the speed of rotation in a machine that has an electric motor, such as an electric mixer. They are also used in car speedometers and lawn sprinklers.

SPUR GEAR

HELICAL GEAR

BEVEL GEAR

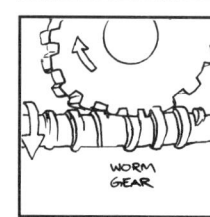
WORM GEAR

Find Out

Use reference books and encyclopedias to find the names and dates of early bicycles. Make drawings of these models and give the names of their inventors. What early bicycle did not use gears? What problems did this cause?

Fold